MASTERING the
CURRENCY
MARKET

MASTERING the CURRENCY MARKET

Forex Strategies for High- and Low-Volatility Markets

JAY NORRIS / AL GASKILL / TERESA BELL

New York   Chicago   San Francisco   Lisbon   London
Madrid   Mexico City   Milan   New Delhi   San Juan
Seoul   Singapore   Sydney   Toronto

ISBN: 978–0–07–163484–7
MHID: 0–07–163484–3

This publication is designed to provide accurate and authoritative information in regard to the subject matter covered. It is sold with the understanding that the publisher is not engaged in rendering legal, accounting, or other professional service. If legal advice or other expert assistance is required, the services of a competent professional person should be sought.

> —*From a declaration of principles jointly adopted by a committee of the American Bar Association and a committee of publishers.*

McGraw-Hill books are available at special quantity discounts to use as premiums and sales promotions, or for use in corporate training programs. To contact a representative please visit the Contact Us pages at www.mhprofessional.com.

CONTENTS

PREFACE

Regardless of your level of economic or market knowledge, the only way to learn how to trade the financial markets successfully is to know the basics and practice using them regularly. We often hear clients say they already know the beginning lessons and believe that the intermediate and advanced lessons will make them successful traders. What we've found in practice, however, is that most individuals lack a complete understanding of the basics.

If you feel you are the exception to this rule, you may want to consider the following questions: Have you written out a trading plan? Do you know the difference between a countertrend signal and a trend signal? Do you understand the concept and timing of buying strength and selling weakness? Do you know that as an end-of-day trader, your risk-to-reward ratio is much more favorable than that of a day trader? Do you understand the difference between a leading and a lagging technical indicator and know how and when to employ them? These are basic lessons you need to know, and if you do not have them hardwired into your head, you very likely will not succeed at trading. Your success will depend on how seriously you take yourself and trading. It's fair to say that any profession that encourages the use of simulators should be taken seriously, and trading is no exception.

The key in many top-earning professions is repetitive practice. Why do you think professional athlete practices as much as they do? Why do you think a middle linebacker or a quarterback who makes millions of dollars a year practices basic footwork so often or why a concert pianist or violinist practices so often? Conditioning is the answer. Professionals condition themselves to react physically the same way, every time, in various situations regardless of their emotions. Professionals make the time and take the effort to practice the basics because they know they have to take themselves out of the process mentally to the point where they don't think, they just react. What may take many years to learn lesson by lesson, with hours, then weeks, and then years of practice, can be executed simply and flawlessly without apparent effort when a professional is in the right place at the right time. We are going to give you the tools and the lessons you need and teach you how to recognize when the time and place are right for you to execute your trading plan.

Why should you think that you can learn to trade when so many people fail at it? Before you picked up this book, the odds were only 1 in 10 that you would succeed. Regardless of how you answered this question, the more important question is, Do you really believe your answer? At the core of your being, do you believe you can learn to trade successfully? That question is the key, because until you possess a fundamental belief that you can do it, you will not have the nerve to take the risks you need to take at the times you need to take them to be a successful trader. Beyond the psychology of trading, we are here to teach you a trading method that once studied, back tested, and demo traded will give you the confidence to both analyze markets and execute trades successfully regardless of the underlying market conditions. Becoming a successful trader gives you freedom. That means that after completing this book and executing what you've been taught, at the same time exhibiting both patience and discipline, you should be able to prove to yourself in a demonstration trading account that you have the knowledge and ability to increase your account size consistently by trading the financial markets. Once you prove this to yourself and become more comfortable with your new skills, there is virtually no limit to how much you can earn over the coming years.

We are very confident in our teaching because of the experience that lies behind our method. In the early 1990s our head trader, Al Gaskill, paid his first technical analysis instructor $5,000 a day to teach him how to use technical indicators. It was money well spent. Over the years we have studied under some of the best trading instructors in the business and always have walked away with valuable knowledge. Whether it was dismissing something that did not work for us or finding something that did, it was always worth the cost of the lessons. Never has that been clearer to us than in today's volatile financial marketplace. In 2008 we saw some of the most volatile markets ever in currency trading, but during that time Al had one of his best years and his most productive period ever—August to October 2008— by using the methods outlined in this book.

We feel very strongly that the currency markets constitute the best trading vehicle in the financial markets right now and will continue to do so. A currency pair is similar to a government bill or note in that it pays or charges interest, depending on whether you are long or short, on the basis of the underlying countries' short-term interest rates. A currency pair trades or behaves like a stock pair, with those underlying interest rates acting as a dividend to traders holding the higher-yielding currency. From a trader's perspective it is a better trading vehicle than an individual country's government securities because of the low cost of entry afforded by margin, the dynamic pricing resulting from the competitive marketplace, and the ease of entry and exit. Though currency pairs trade or behave similarly to international stock funds, the cost is much, much lower and the overall risk is lower as well. We acknowledge that being long or short the Australian dollar and simultaneously short or long the Japanese yen can be a risky endeavor, particularly on margin; however, we always encourage the use of stop-loss orders, and in comparison to stocks, you don't have to worry about a currency pair evaporating, as happened to some of the old-guard Wall Street firms that were trading stocks in 2008.

With the leveling out of international markets by globalization and the increased level of competition this has bred, the growth of trading in the foreign exchange market—forex—is virtually assured as both professional and retail investors realize the advantages of this market over investing and trading traditional stocks, stock indexes, and securities markets.

You will learn that to be a successful trader is to be a man or woman for all seasons. It means independence, but more than that it means having a quiet confidence in what the future holds. Well-rounded traders know they can make money regardless of the underlying fundamentals or overriding realities. The more volatile markets become—that is, the faster a market moves—the faster a trader can make money. Equally, when a market slows down, a trader downshifts to countertrending methods. Regardless of the certainty or uncertainty of economic conditions, markets will move and astute traders will benefit. With so many experienced financial leaders and commentators pointing to a sustained recession for years to come, it is not a question of whether traders will be successful; it is a matter of how successful in light of the levels of economic uncertainty in the current financial marketplace.

There is definitely a dark side to trading. People lose, and losing is stressful. Trading certainly can be stressful, but when it is taught in a supportive environment, studied thoroughly, and practiced on a regular basis, the decision-making process involved in trading can be a healthy development. The way to avoid the stress and ease the learning curve for as long as it takes, is to demo trade: open a practice or simulation account. We highly recommend that you open a demonstration account and promise yourself that you will not risk live money until you've proved to yourself that you consistently can show a profit in the demo account. When you get to that point of consistency, you will have shown a level of patience and discipline that can pay handsome dividends not just in trading but in life.

Before you venture too far into this book, we need to cover the physiological impact trading will have. Your nervous system is going to work against you as a trader. As part of our physical makeup, we all have what is called the autonomic nervous system, which regulates subconscious biological functions such as heartbeat, digestive processes, perspiration, and vision. Within the autonomic nervous system are the sympathetic and parasympathetic branches. The sympathetic branch is what we rely on when we are angry or afraid. It is what increases our heartbeat and adrenaline flow during times of stress, making us literally jumpy. This physical change is also what we call the fight or flight response, which was useful 10,000 years ago when people lived in caves but today can make for a very tough learning environment. The excitement of making seemingly easy money, followed, sometimes just seconds later, by fear of loss and failure will break most people down quickly. The emotional ups and downs we create in our minds, followed by the physical changes in our blood pressure and adrenal glands, make for a tough environment in which to learn and then retain knowledge. The automatic fight or flight response hardwired into your head will work against you as a trader. There will be times when you click the mouse to enter or exit a trade and instantly ask yourself, "Why did I do that?" because you realize you are not following your trading plan. Before you get angry at yourself, realize that you are not the only trader who ever let emotion override logic. In fact, you are programmed to react that way.

Luckily for us, along with the fight or flight function regulated by the sympathetic branch of the autonomic nervous system, there is the parasympathetic branch, which can have a calming effect on us and our bodies. It is this sympathetic branch that we want to stimulate as we are learning and studying trading lessons. You will get the most out of this book by studying it in a relaxed and pleasant atmosphere. If you currently are trading, you should consider taking a break from it while you study this material. Learn what stimulates the sympathetic branch of the autonomic nervous system and engage in that activity before studying this material and again afterward. Get in the habit of taking care of your mind and body in this way until it is habitual. You will find that by taking the time to put yourself in a relaxed, meditative state before starting your day and again before quitting in the evening, you will remain much calmer and more focused than the millions of other people online who are risking their hard-earned money every day in the marketplace.

JAY NORRIS

MASTERING the
CURRENCY
MARKET

PART 1

INTRODUCTION TO TRADING CURRENCIES

CHAPTER 1

TYPES OF FINANCIAL MARKETS

M arkets generally are classified by type. The capital markets consist of the stock and bond markets, which have instruments that may be traded on the New York Stock Exchange (NYSE). There are also commodities and derivatives markets, which feature financial products that are based on the underlying commodities and are traded on central exchanges such as the Chicago Mercantile Exchange. The markets on which this book will focus are the financial markets, the foreign exchange market, or forex, in particular.

Risk versus Reward

Before beginning an investing or trading program, it is very important to understand the concept of risk versus reward. All investments carry some degree of risk; there is no such thing as a zero-risk investment. Higher potential rewards almost always are coupled with higher risk. Figure 1-1 shows an

Low Risk	Limited Risk	Moderate Risk	High Risk
Treasury Bonds	Blue Chip Stocks	Growth Stocks	Futures
Treasury Bills	High-Rated Corporate Bonds	Low-Rated Corporate Bonds	Speculative Stocks
Bank CDs	High-Rated Municipal Bonds	International Investments	High-Yield Bonds
Money Market Funds	Balanced Mutual Funds		Forex

Figure 1-1 Risk Aversion Table

investment spectrum of low-risk and high-risk options. The markets this book will cover are considered a high-risk investment. We do not recommend a high-risk investment strategy for any money you cannot afford to lose. Risk can include factors, such as inflation and recessions, that affect the value of what you are holding.

Methods That Apply to Multiple Markets

The methods we will be discussing apply to all markets, including stocks, bonds, futures, options, and forex. Because of the liquidity of the international currency markets, the low cost of entry, and the advent of easy-to-use platforms and free charting packages, along with mini and micro contracts, most of the examples we give will be in the forex markets.

Foreign Currency Trading

Foreign currency trading on a retail level was the brainchild of Leo Melamed, chairman emeritus of the Chicago Mercantile Exchange, with encouragement from the economist and Nobel laureate Milton Friedman. In 1972 the Chicago Mercantile Exchange started trading futures that were based on the exchange rate between the U.S. dollar and other major currencies, and the growth in financial derivatives has not slowed since that time.

Foreign exchange trading was nothing new to banks and large institutions, and it wasn't long before brokers and dealers around the world devised ways to make markets outside the central location of the futures market in Chicago. The name *forex* is an abbreviation for the words "foreign exchange." Worldwide, the forex market is the most actively traded financial market. The daily volume on the forex market is equal to three to four times that of all other markets combined, with an average daily turnover of $3.2 trillion. Forex is an extremely liquid market because of the high level of participation, or high volume, and the fact that currencies have a tendency to move in sustained trends relative to other markets or investments. Liquidity is important if one wants to be able to get in and out of a market quickly, and when we study trending markets, you will see that strong trends represent opportunities to make a lot of money if you are on the right side of the trade. Forex is traded 24 hours a day during the workweek, closing Friday at 5 p.m. Eastern Standard Time and reopening Sunday at 5 p.m. Forex also has a low cost of entry; an investor can open an account with as little as $250.

Currency Trading History

Here are the highlights of the history of currency trading.

- When currency systems were introduced, a country's currency value was set against a gold standard.

- In times of rapid political and economic change, the gold standard becomes a problem. Therefore, after World War I and World War II, many countries abandoned the gold standard and adopted the Bretton Woods Accord.
- Between 1944 and 1971, exchange rates for foreign currencies were set at a price fixed against the U.S. dollar.
- In December 1971, the Bretton Woods Accord that had established the fixed rates was abandoned, and several other systems were implemented briefly before a floating exchange system was established.
- In 1972, the Chicago Mercantile Exchange starting trading currency futures.
- At present, the currencies of most countries are valued relative to the value of other currencies.
- With the expansion of the World Wide Web, the forex market has been opened to include speculators and private investors.

Forex Basics

As we mentioned previously, the forex market is traded 24 hours a day during the workweek and closes on Friday at 5 p.m. EST. Figure 1-2 shows the opening and closing times. The hours are adjusted in the United States during Daylight Savings Time.

What Is Traded on Forex?

Almost all the transactions on the forex market involve currency pairs. However, it is possible to trade precious metals through most foreign exchange dealers.

Time Zone	New York	GMT
Tokyo Open	7:00 p.m.	0:00
Tokyo Close	4:00 a.m.	9:00
London Open	3:00 a.m.	8:00
London Close	12:00 p.m.	17:00
New York Open	8:00 a.m.	13:00
New York Close	5:00 p.m.	22:00

Figure 1-2 Global Trading Hours Schedule

The Six Majors

GBPUSD   AUDUSD   EURUSD
USDCAD   USDJPY   USDCHF

The most commonly traded currency pairs on the forex market are called the six majors. They are the British pound (GBPUSD, also known as "sterling" or the "cable"), the Canadian dollar (USDCAD, aka the "looney"), the Australian dollar (AUDUSD, aka the "Aussie"), the Japanese yen (USDJPY, aka the "yen"), the euro (EURUSD, aka the "fiber"), and the Swiss franc (USDCHF, aka the "Swissy" or "chief") (see Figure 1-3).

Distribution by Currency Pair

It is estimated that the U.S. dollar is involved in over 70 percent of all transactions on the forex markets. Figure 1-4 shows the breakdown of volume traded for the major currency pairs.

Examples
AUDCAD   AUDNZD   GBPJPY
Cross Currency Pairs   *EURJPY   EURCHF   CADJPY*

Cross currency pairs (see Figure 1-5) are those which do not involve the U.S. dollar. They tend to trade at lower volume, and the spreads are usually higher for these pairs than for the

7

The Majors

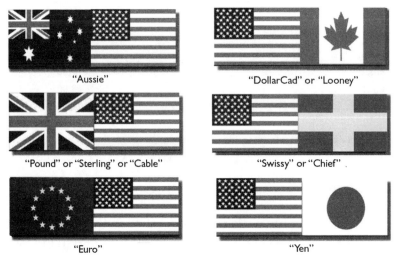

"Aussie"

"DollarCad" or "Looney"

"Pound" or "Sterling" or "Cable"

"Swissy" or "Chief"

"Euro"

"Yen"

Figure 1-3 Major Currency Pairs

Estimated Trading Volume by Currency Pair

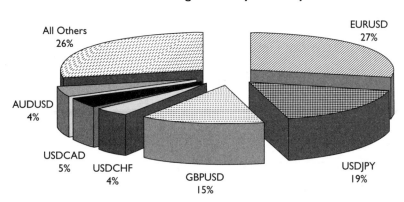

Figure 1-4 Approximate Volume Breakdown per Currency Pair

Cross Currency Pairs

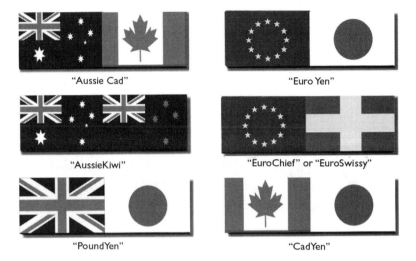

"Aussie Cad"   "Euro Yen"

"AussieKiwi"   "EuroChief" or "EuroSwissy"

"PoundYen"   "CadYen"

Figure 1-5 Examples of Cross Currency Pairs

majors. An exception to this rule are pairs such as the euroyen (EURJPY) and euroswiss (EURCHF), which offer tight spreads and excellent trading opportunities. Examples of cross currency pairs include Canadian dollar/Japanese yen = CADJPY, New Zealand dollar/Japanese yen = NZDJPY, euro/Japanese yen = EURJPY, and British pound/Japanese yen = GBPJPY. In Chapter 2 we discuss in more detail the contribution of the major currencies to the global marketplace.

Understanding Currency Pairs

Currency prices are quoted relative to another currency's price as a result of constantly fluctuating values. In each currency

```
XXX / YYY
XXX is the "base" currency
and
YYY is the "counter" currency
```

Figure 1-6 Base Currency versus Counter Currency

pair (see Figure 1-6), the first currency listed is the *base* currency and always has a value of 1.0. The second currency listed is the *counter* currency. For example, EURUSD is the value of the euro expressed in U.S. dollars.

Understanding Currency Values

The following example shows how fluctuations affect currency prices:

- *USD/JPY 110.08* means that 1 U.S. dollar equals 110.08 Japanese yen.
- If the price moves to *USD/JPY 111.08*, it means that the dollar has gotten stronger, as one could buy more yen per dollar.
- Conversely, if the price moves to *USD/JPY 109.08*, the dollar has gotten weaker, as it buys fewer yen per dollar.
- Prices for the JPY are given to two decimal places, but prices for all other currencies are given to four decimal places.

What Is a Pip?

A pip (Figure 1-7) is the smallest value by which a currency may fluctuate in the forex market. *Pip* stands for "price in percentage" and sometimes is referred to as a "tick." Let us see how this works.

- A move from EUR/USD 1.5555 to 1.5550 is referred to as a 5-pip move.
- A move from USD/JPY 113.00 to 113.05 also is referred to as a 5-pip move, since the yen is recorded only out to two decimal places.

It is a good idea to do the math and know what a pip equates to in terms of the base currency one is trading. For most scenarios, the pip is equal to 0.0001, or 0.01 percent. In

Understanding PIPs

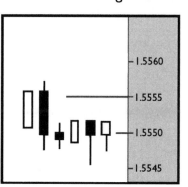

Figure 1-7 Minimum Price Fluctuations

```
              Sample PIP Calculation
            Exchange rate = 119.90
              Lot size = $100,000
      (0.1/119.80) × $100,000 = $8.34 per pip
```

Figure 1-8   Pip Calculation to Determine Monetary Value

that case the formula is (0.0001/exchange rate) × contract size (see Figure 1-8).

Lot Sizes

A standard currency contract is referred to as a *lot*. Initially, lot sizes were very large because currencies were traded only by large financial institutions. As the "retail" sector of the forex market opened up, the market came up with smaller units called mini lots and micro lots. Figure 1-9 lists their values. With the advent of smaller lot sizes, the market has been opened up to a larger number of individuals.

Standard	$100,000
Mini	$10,000
Micro	$1,000

Figure 1-9   Forex Contract Sizes

Bid and Ask Prices

The ask price is the price at which a trader will buy the base currency in exchange for the counter currency. The bid price is the price at which a trader will sell the base currency in exchange for the counter currency. The bid price is always lower than the ask price. Figure 1-10 shows how the bid and ask prices equal the spread.

The Spread

The spread is the difference between the bid price and the ask price. Figure 1-11 shows how the spread is calculated. The spread is the compensation a broker receives for every

---

Understanding Currency Quotes

EURUSD 1.5545/1.5547

Bid = 1.5545
Ask = 1.5547

Figure 1-10 Bid and Ask Prices = Spread

Calculating the Spread

EURUSD 1.5545/1.5547

Bid = 1.5545
Ask = 1.5547

Spread = 1.5547−1.5545 = .0002 = 2 pip

Figure 1-11 Spread = Transactional Cost

transaction an investor places. Spreads are usually fairly "tight" for the major currency pairs, but they can be considerably higher for cross currency pairs. This is one reason we do not recommend trading cross currency pairs except in a long-term position trade; the costs may be too high to make it consistently profitable.

Understanding Leverage

Leverage is the factor that makes forex trading both high-risk and high-reward. You put up only a portion of the amount traded and then can trade up to 200 times the value of your account. With leverage, the total value of your account can increase faster and also can be wiped out much faster. Start slowly with leverage and then move up your ratios slowly as you gain experience. We will talk about this concept in the section on money management. A limited number of brokers also offer leverage of up to 400 times the value of an account. We do not recommend ever using that much leverage. You do not want to risk more than the value of your account; for the most part there are no margin calls, and the broker will close out all your positions to avoid incurring a debit balance. You can lose your entire account very quickly if it is highly leveraged. Although some dealers and forex brokers give their clients assurances that they cannot lose more money than they have in the account, if there is a cataclysmic event, those assurances may not hold up. It is crucial that you understand risk and follow the rules necessary to limit your downside risk. Many errors in forex are due to failure to follow the established rules.

Margin Calls

When your account has leverage, the total dollar value of the currency you control is much larger than the value of your account. For example, if you have an account that is leveraged 200:1, a $1,000 balance controls $200,000 worth of currency. Your account is worth 1/200, or one-half of a percent, of the contract you control. That means that if the underlying currency moves by 0.5 percent and you are on the wrong side of the move, your account value will go down to zero. Conversely, if you are on the right side of the move and the currency moves to the same degree, your account value will double. It is a double-edged sword. If your account value falls to zero, the broker or dealer will try to close out your position to avoid a debit balance. In other financial markets the practice has been for the broker to make a call to the customer to see if the customer would like to put up extra margin to stay in his or her position, hoping that things will turn around. Our philosophy on margins calls is "never answer a margin call," and with most forex brokers you don't have a choice. They try to close your position out for you before the account goes into debit. If they do not close it out in time, however, you will incur the debt.

Minimizing Risk

We talk in greater detail about minimizing risk in the section on money management. Before you get started, though, there are some basic rules about risk that you need to know and observe:

- We recommend practicing with a demo account before trading a "live" account.
- Develop your confidence and skills on a demo account or micro account, and once you have developed a good track record, switch to a live account.
- Always monitor your positions actively.
- Never hold a position without an accompanying stop-loss order. This is an order that is based on how much you are willing to risk on the trade. If you have a 200-pip stop order, once the trade moves 200 pips against you, the position is closed automatically.
- Never risk more than 5 percent of the value of your account on one transaction.
- Have a trading plan that outlines your entry and exit strategies. We will show you how to build a trading plan in Chapter 13.
- Follow your trading plan.

Forex versus Futures

For professional investors, there are a couple of distinct advantages to trading currency futures contracts. First, traders who use currency futures are assured that their funds are placed in a bank account segregated from the dealing firm's money; this is different from the practice of many foreign exchange dealers, in which the client's and the dealer's money often are commingled. Futures also ensure lower transactions costs because the markup between the bid and the offer is determined by professional traders and market makers who participate in the transparent and very competitive world of futures trading, not by individual banks and dealers who generally mark up the spread to wider levels. It is through this spread that forex dealers are compensated. Although forex dealers have had to respond with tighter spreads for their clients over the last year or so, these advantages still generally lie with futures markets: Futures still maintain a tighter spread between the bid and the offer, and futures clients have negotiated their commission to well below the minimum tick value that represents the smallest increment in which the price can move.

On any given day the Chicago Mercantile Exchange (CME) trades over 400,000 currency futures contracts for a face value of over $400 billion in business. However, because of larger account minimums, larger contract sizes, higher margin rates, and government regulations, the futures markets have taken a backseat to the growth of the underregulated cash currency markets, or forex, over the last 10 years. In futures markets, traders compete among themselves and with market makers around the clock, with all the participants having access to the same tight bid and offer, or spread, that is created in a central marketplace regulated by the National Futures Association, whereas traders in forex compete directly with the dealer. The dealer shows the client what is known as a retail spread, whereas the dealer has excess to an institutional spread and the futures spread, which are generally tighter than the retail forex spread. This difference between the retail spread and the institutional spread is profitable for forex dealers, particularly since a high percentage of the participants trading with the dealer are not professionals. Having this distinct advantage, along with the Internet to promote their services, dealers spend a good percentage of their profits on upgrading their state-of-the-art trading platforms and charting packages to entice clients to trade with them.

These efforts by the dealers to improve their order delivery platforms and charting and analysis packages can benefit educated clients. Another advantage for clients who choose to trade with a forex dealer is the smaller contract sizes. One of the main reasons retail clients lose money trading is that they risk too much per transaction. In futures the minimum contract size is $62,500, whereas in forex it is just $1,000 for a micro contract and $10,000 for a mini contract. With these smaller contracts, it is much easier for a retail client to manage and maintain acceptable trading risk-reward ratios than it would be with the larger futures contracts. Because of the ease of trade management the smaller forex contracts afford, particularly the fact that a trader can keep the risk per trade to a fixed percentage of his or her account size, we will focus primarily on the forex markets. If you are inexperienced in trading, especially in trading forex, keep in mind that it is a very serious business. The dealers are in business to capture the transactional costs generated by your trading. You are in business to make money trading. You need to understand this duality: Information you receive directly or indirectly from a dealer is geared toward getting you to trade more to generate the transactional costs created by the spread.

PART 2

FUNDAMENTAL ANALYSIS

CHAPTER 2

THE WHY OF PRICE VALUATION

Fundamental analysis focuses on the why of price valuation for a stock, an index, or a currency. Multiple factors affect the value of an asset or market, and in this part of the book we attempt to explain those factors in simplified terms. We need to be aware that fundamentals move the market on both the short-term and long-term levels because that can provide the basis for a trading decision. However, when it comes to execution, which involves the when and the how in the trading equation, we rely on additional information to supplement the fundamentals.

Fundamental analysis historically has been used to evaluate the worth of a company by valuing its stock price. As we have seen new markets emerge and new financial instruments develop, fundamental analysis has been used to price those markets and instruments as well. When applied to the forex market, fundamental analysis has a twofold purpose: determining the short-term impact on currency prices and forecasting long-term trends. We will examine some of the underlying forces that affect fundamentals. We've chosen to focus on U.S. fundamentals because the U.S. dollar is involved in approximately 70 percent of currency transactions. The overall generalizations we make about U.S. economic indicators and U.S. interest rates apply in the same manner to other countries' fundamentals and interest rates in relation to their currency valuations. Keep in mind that currency trading is relative from currency to currency and economy to economy as the business cycle evolves. When it comes to buying and selling currencies at different times in the global business cycle, it is not about identifying the strongest currency so much as it is a matter of identifying the least weak currency.

Effect of the Business Climate

The same forces that affect the value of a business have an impact on the price of currencies. In fundamental terms, a company is valued on the basis of its balance sheet and current or future income as well as intangible factors that will affect that future income, including business model and plan, management and leadership, competitive advantage, and adherence to laws and regulations. External factors that affect a company's value include the valuation of the industry in which it competes, the company's rank or market share in that industry, interest rates, and current or pending legislation that will affect regulation of the industry. If a company's products or services are selling at a profit and are expected to continue doing that and if other market conditions are favorable, that company's value, or stock, should go up. It is said that the company is fundamentally sound in those circumstances, and the market reflects that value. If sales slow, expenses are higher than expected, or external factors affecting profitability change in a negative direction, the stock price should go down. If sales are steady and the company makes no appreciable gains, the stock may go sideways.

Similar concepts apply to countries and geographic unions. In very simplified terms, if the companies and citizens in a country are producing more than they spend and taxes are sufficient to cover expenses, increased income in the form of tax receipts flows into government coffers. Because most businesses continually seek to improve, there is increased competition for money, or funding, as individuals and businesses borrow money to expand. An increased rate of borrowing money leads to increases in interest rates, which will attract capital from investors seeking a higher yield for their savings and investments and thus cause an increase in tax receipts. Job growth is healthy when businesses are spending money to stay competitive. In a healthy worldwide environment, the stronger an individual country's economy is, the more demand there is for stocks and other investments denominated in that currency, the more pressure there is for higher interest rates, and the stronger the currency is. Conversely, the slower the economy is, the more pressure it puts on stock prices as investors exit investments in search of higher yields and on central bankers to lower interest rates, further decreasing the return on investments valued in that country's currency; in that case, the country's currency becomes weaker.

To generalize about the impact of a positive global business climate, it can be said that higher interest rates mean a stronger currency and that a weaker currency leads to lower interest rates. The most direct link between interest rates and currency values is the level of business activity. If business activity is growing, there is room for higher interest rates created by demand for more money and thus a stronger currency. If business activity is contracting, higher interest rates are a threat to commerce and interest rates may have to be lowered, with the effect being a weaker currency.

In times of global economic uncertainty and recession, however, traders and investors favor lower-yielding currencies because governments and businesses in those countries will be relatively less handicapped by lower borrowing costs (interest rates) in a slowing economic environment. In summer 2008 we saw a good example of this as global stock markets turned lower, erasing the gains of the previous two years. Investors around the world went from thinking about the return *on* their investments to being concerned about the return *of* their investments. With governments, businesses, and individuals all trying to exit their previously higher-yielding investments at the same time, currencies with higher-yielding interest rates fell sharply as money poured out of the British, European, Canadian, Australian, and New Zealand currencies and into the lower-yielding U.S. dollar and Japanese yen. The sharp reevaluation of currencies in the third and fourth quarters of 2008 also pointed out the fact that the currency market is a self-correcting mechanism. What strengthens a currency initially also can weaken it as interest rates become too high and currency valuations become too inflated relative to those of competing countries and unions.

Although Canadian citizens felt proud as their currency rose from 0.60 to 0.80 against that of their U.S. neighbors, Canadian businesspeople felt concern and then fear as the looney kept on strengthening from 0.80 to 1.00 against, or on par with, the U.S. currency. This 40 percent increase in the looney made it very easy for American farmers and manufacturers to take business from their Canadian counterparts because the cost of American feed and products was so much lower compared with the Canadian than it had been just three or four years earlier. As business shifted away from Canada, the looney turned and was sold off, and the Canadian government cut interest rates accordingly. Like a pendulum that has swung too far, it can be said that the weight of a stronger currency can cause its value to swing lower. It is this characteristic of a free enterprise system with floating currency values that ideally ensures that the best products and services at the most competitive prices are what will set economic standards going forward, not political or nationalistic considerations.

Interest Rates and the Carry Trade

As we saw with regard to the effects the overall business environment has on currencies, interest rates play a key role. One way to take advantage of interest rate differentials between countries is by buying a currency with a higher interest rate and collecting that interest and then selling a currency with a lower interest rate; when the short position pays the interest rate, this is called the carry trade. In times of global economic expansion, investors and traders make money by using this strategy.

A typical example from a couple of years ago would be buying U.S. dollars and selling Japanese yen; in trading parlance this is known as going long USDJPY. If interest rates were 3.0 percent in the United States and 0.5 percent in Japan, the position would yield, or "carry," an annual rate of 2.5 percent. If the trader had on a position of long five standard lots, or $500,000, he would collect 2.5 percent annually on the $500,000 even if he had only $10,000 in his account. That may sound like a lot of money at first, but consider the risk that individual would be incurring to capture that $35 a day in interest. By holding a $500,000 position in a $10,000 account, the trader could lose everything if USDJPY moved just 2 percent. In today's marketplace a 2 percent move in a single day for a currency pair is not unreasonable. In a much larger account, in a healthy economic climate, and with the account managed by professionals, this arbitrage strategy makes a lot of sense. Professional traders understand this and have taken advantage of interest rate differentials in the global marketplace during times of economic expansion. For an individual with little experience and a small account, the strategy is inadvisable and dangerous.

The last time the carry trade was working, from mid-2005 to mid-2007, it was working very well. Prices of the higher-yielding currencies raced higher while prices of the lower-yielding currencies stood still or even moved lower. What this meant was not only that buyers, or "longs," in the carry trade were capturing the interest on their positions but that they were reaping the traders' reward as their positions increased in value. Individuals with little experience were accumulating larger and larger long positions and calling themselves traders. You probably can guess how this ended. Prices plummeted violently at the beginning of 2008 as speculative monies vanished when stock and real estate markets fell sharply after their inflated advances earlier in the decade. After a long pause through the spring and early summer of 2008, the sell-off accelerated again in mid-2008 as carry traders with only a few years' experience learned the hard way that what goes up comes down. They also learned that earning a few pips a day on a carry trade was not trading at all. The bright side of this situation for experienced traders was that after the carry trade evaporated, two-way trade resumed. After the majority of the speculative money was wiped out, prices were free to move up and down, which is what markets do in normal conditions.

Inflation and Commodities

An important link between interest rates and currency values is commodity inflation, which, unlike an individual area or country's business activity, affects all economies. As inflation rises and prices spiral upward, some people quickly start to buy up future supplies of basic necessities as insurance against higher prices in the future. In that scenario, prices go up not because of healthy business activity but because of uncertainty and fear—and fear moves markets. In that scenario the government can increase the interest rate earned on cash deposits to get individuals to sell off their stockpiles of supplies in exchange for cash and the increased dividend created by higher interest rates. This seems a responsible action but does not work in all cases. Some individuals are inclined to hang on to their supplies rather than take the cash, and attempts at easing inflation can be thwarted.

Businesses and economies around the world wrestled with a very similar fundamental problem with the supply of crude oil from 2005 through 2008. Crude supplies were shrinking as worldwide demand increased, and that caused the price of crude to jump from under $40 per barrel in 2004 to a high of $140 in July 2008. That created additional expenses and commodity shortages and the fundamental complications that go along with that situation. Those problems had not been in place just a few years before. Countries that had their own supplies of crude didn't feel the need to raise interest rates, whereas some countries and regions that did not have their own supplies did. The interest rate differentials created opportunities for traders but caused much confusion for the economists and politicians charged with solving those complex problems.

Generally, a rise in commodity inflation will cause a rise in the value of the currency of a country that has large supplies of that commodity. Again, however, it is important to keep in mind that currency valuations are relative. Many analysts and commentators called the Canadian and Australian currencies commodity currencies because those countries have an abundant supply of commodities, and as the price of commodities moved higher from 2002 through 2008, so did those two currencies. The United States also has an abundance of commodities, whereas Switzerland does not, yet the U.S. currency went down and the Swiss currency increased sharply over that period. This leads to the question, was there really a relationship between commodities going up and these so-called commodity currencies going up, or did they just happen to be different investment classes that were going up at the same time? As it turned out, the Canadian currency topped out a full seven months before crude oil peaked, whereas gold peaked four months ahead of the Australian dollar. As of December 2008, gold was off its all-time high by just 15 percent and the Australian currency was off its high by 30 percent.

We believe that both commodities and currencies are complex vehicles that should be traded individually on the basis of price movement. There are relationships between different markets and asset classes, but relationships by definition change, particularly when one is comparing complex pricing processes such as commodities and currencies. "Don't get caught trading wheat in the corn pit" is an old Chicago trading adage. It can be said that the same thing is true when one is trading a currency that is based on a commodity's price or vice versa.

Commodity inflation overall adds uncertainty to markets as governments try to offset the effects of rising and falling prices with interest rate or other policy changes when often it is best to let the markets correct themselves. Uncertainty in the markets produces price movement, which is always beneficial for traders.

Consumer Habits

One also must take into account the effects that prosperity and the appearance of continued prosperity have on financial markets; this also is known as the boom-bust cycle. When economies are strong, such as that of the United States in the 1990s and from 2003 through 2007, it creates the expectation that strong economic growth will continue. As is often the case in economics and markets, the seeds for the downturn were created by overoptimism during the upturn, as stocks were bid up to unreasonably inflated valuations in the late 1990s, followed by the same phenomenon in real estate in the 2000s. "Chicken today, feathers tomorrow," as the old saying goes. That means, "Don't worry about tomorrow; get what you want today." This is a classic behavioral mannerism of many young adults during the first half of their employment cycle. For many, it does not make fundamental sense to drive a large motor vehicle that gets poor gas mileage or to take on a large home and mortgage in anticipation of a promotion and monetary raise the next year.

More often than not, this leveraging of the future to get more of a good thing in the present leads consumers to tip over financially. The newspapers were full of these types of stories in 2007 and early 2008, and they projected economic slowdowns after extended periods of excess. The fact that many people have excessive debt is projected to weigh on consumer spending and therefore on business spending. The drying up of consumer spending can affect a country's currency, and when the behavior is collective, the whole global marketplace can feel the pinch. Excessive consumer spending without the earnings to pay for it leads to a downward spiral brought on by debt and unsound economic decisions made by countries' primary consumers.

On a microeconomic level individuals are responsible for their own finances, but on a macroeconomic level people look to governing bodies for help in a financial crisis. This is what happened in the second half of 2008 and the beginning of 2009. Governments embarked on a policy of notching down interest rates so that they could attempt to borrow their way out of trouble by lending to and buying into industries and companies hurt by the uncertainty and fear created by falling stock prices and ane-mic consumer and business spending. As of this writing, the jury is still out on this strategy of governments keeping businesses and industries afloat to ensure both employment and a tax base and stabilize corporate securities markets. The thing to remember as traders is that we do not attempt to anticipate the effects of this strategy in the financial marketplace. We let the market tell us how it interprets these actions by seeing which signals are proving profitable, the buy triggers or the sell triggers. We do know this, though: The volatility created by economic uncertainty is a feeding bell for professional traders.

There are many nuances in the fundamental valuations of stocks, other financial instruments, and currencies, and we've taken a look at the major ones. As we've seen, there are four important factors in the pricing process for financial markets:

1. Current business conditions, meaning income and cash on hand for companies
2. Interest rates, in which differentials between countries can create market momentum
3. Inflation, in which the concern is whether inflation is growing or ebbing
4. Individual spending habits, which are defined as housing and disposable income

The bottom line in business and market valuations nearly always is determined by fundamental developments. Fundamentals are the why of price action. There is no doubt about the role a country or region's capital flows and trade flows play in determining currency prices.

Below, we summarize the key economic reports and discuss their impact on currency prices.

Key Economic Reports

Fundamental traders, economists, and market analysts gauge economic activity by studying and interpreting economic reports and readings released by companies and government agencies. These news releases are available at a number of online sites. We use www.ForexFactory.com, which is one of the leading sites in the forex industry for news. On the front page of its Web site there is a tab for "Calendar." If you click on that tab, it will show an extended list of economic releases for the week and their expected impact. Releases with a red icon have the highest expected level of impact. Another great resource is www.munibondadvisor.com/EconomicIndicators.htm, which links readers directly to the source for every news release.

Figure 2-1 shows a summary spreadsheet of the most influential news releases for the United States, including the typical release dates and the net effect a release may have on the U.S. dollar. Note that these are generalizations and cover only one factor affecting currency prices. We do not recommend that anyone trade ahead of a major news release, as the results can be extreme and unpredictable.

The way traders react to these economic reports and releases is always dynamic, and that is why they are covered extensively on the financial news shows. Economic reports can reinforce the existing trend as related releases confirm one another, or the reports can contradict one another, which could indicate

Key Economic Reports

Report	Change	Dollar Friendly	Dollar Unfriendly	Release Date
Non-Farm Payroll	Payroll increases	X		The first Friday of every month at 8:30 a.m. EST
	Payroll decreases		X	
FOMC	Interest rates increase	X		Release time varies — they meet 8 times per year
	Interest rates decrease		X	
Retail Sales	Sales increase	X		Midmonth, usually around the 13th at 8:30 a.m. EST
	Sales decrease		X	
Durable Goods	Factory orders increase	X		Twice per month at 8:30 a.m. EST
	Factory orders decrease		X	
Gross Domestic Product	Increase in GDP	X		Quarterly on the 25th of the month at 8:30 a.m. EST
	Decrease in GDP		X	
Producer Price Index	Prices increase	X		The third week of each month at 10:00 a.m. EST
	Prices decrease		X	
Consumer Price Index	Prices increase	X		Midmonth at 8:30 a.m. EST
	Prices decrease		X	
Consumer Confidence	Spending increases	X		The last Tuesday of every month at 10:00 a.m. EST
	Spending decreases		X	

Leading Indicators

Report	Change	Dollar Friendly	Dollar Unfriendly
The S&P 500	Index value increases	X	
	Index value decreases		X
U.S. T-Bonds and Notes	Value increases		X
	Value decreases	X	

Figure 2-1 Key Economic Reports and Leading Indicators

33

a possible change in underlying business conditions. The way traders react to the reports in their positioning in the marketplace—their buying and selling—is also a very dynamic process. A report came out that is indisputably market-friendly in a mature up move, and traders may take this as a reason to take a profit and sell. The traders' reasoning may be "We were long this market because of existing favorable conditions, and this report proves our thesis was correct, so let's take some money off the table and put it in our pockets now because we don't know if things can get much better than this." "A bird in the hand is better than two in the bush" is standard operating procedure for many who make a living risking their earnings in the marketplace.

The way traders and markets react to the different fundamental news releases and events is a study in chaos. How many contracts players trade and the direction in which they execute their trades immediately after a fundamental news release may have as much to do with the way they were positioned before the news release as it does with what the actual news told them. Herd mentality also plays a role as influential players may opt to adjust or exit a position more because of the level at which the market is trading than because of the actual fundamental news. A large player making an adjustment to its long-term position can have an outsized effect on a market that may trigger price signals for other traders who operate on shorter-term time frames. Also, there are always times when traders get caught flat-footed after a surprising influential news release and markets make sharp sustained moves, forcing even longer-term traders into exiting positions without as much consideration and time as they would like. Do not expect that after reading a chapter in a book or even reading a series of books you will understand all the factors that affect releases of economic numbers. Over time and through experience, however, you will start to understand these pieces of the puzzle and the way they relate, if at all, to your trading plan. Let's define some significant fundamental releases and see the effects they have on the different markets.

Nonfarm Payroll

The nonfarm payroll reports the amount of jobs added to or subtracted from the U.S. economy in the nonagricultural sectors over the previous month. It is released on the first Friday of the month. It can have an outsized effect on markets because it is considered a very influential reading on economic health. This number is reported by the U.S. Department of Labor, Bureau of Labor Statistics, at www.bls.gov.

Figures 2-2 and 2-3 show the powerful effects of the nonfarm payroll number on June 6, 2008, in both the U.S. stock market and the EURUSD market. The report indicated a sharp drop in payrolls accompanied by a 0.5 percent jump in the unemployment rate and had an outsized effect on stock prices and the U.S. dollar. The Dow Jones Industrial Average fell approximately 400 points, and the euro ended up benefiting from the bad news by pulling out of a downtrend and rallying over 2 points.

The Federal Open Market Committee

The Federal Open Market Committee (FOMC) has considerable influence on all financial markets because it is this governing body of the Federal Reserve Board that sets interest rate policy. The committee reports on interest rate decisions

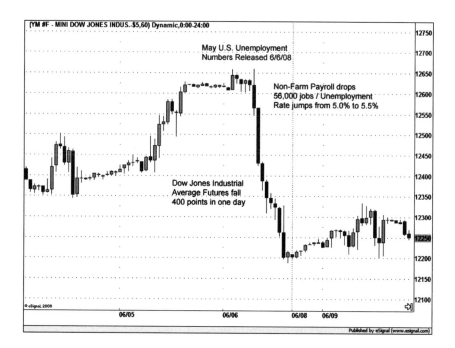

Figure 2-2 Effects of a Higher Than Expected Unemployment Figure on the U.S. Stock Market

by the Federal Reserve Bank (the Fed) and gives traders valuable insights into the Fed's decision-making process through those reports. The committee meets eight times a year, and there is an announcement after the close of each meeting. A change in the federal funds rate (the rate at which banks lend money to each other) as mandated by the Fed affects interest rates across the board and can have a major impact on business decisions across a wide range of businesses and industries. The results for the FOMC meetings are reported on the Federal Reserve Web site at www.federalreserve.gov.

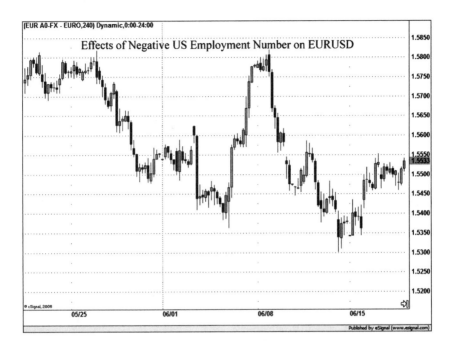

Figure 2-3 Effects of Higher Than Expected Unemployment Figure on EURUSD

Always remember that in general a decision to raise interest rates will be U.S. dollar-friendly and a decision to lower rates will be U.S. dollar-bearish.

Figure 2-4 shows an initially bearish reaction for the dollar as the USDJPY was sold off when the FOMC announced that it would leave interest rates unchanged rather than raise them in the face of rising commodity inflation, as some economists were recommending. In this case the initial knee-jerk reaction lower was short-lived as USDJPY continued on its previous path higher.

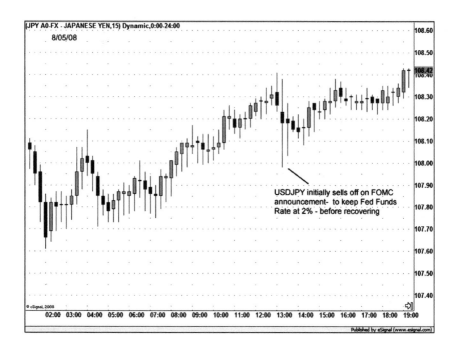

Figure 2-4 Initial Reaction to FOMC Announcement Was Short-Lived

Durable Goods

The monthly report on durable goods indicates the value of orders received by U.S. domestic manufacturers for big-ticket items with a life expectancy of more than three years such as motor vehicles, appliances, and computers. The release comes out at the end of every month and is a compiled from a variety of sources. The figures on durable goods are released by the U.S. Census Bureau and can be found on its Web site at http://www.census.gov/indicator/www/m3/.

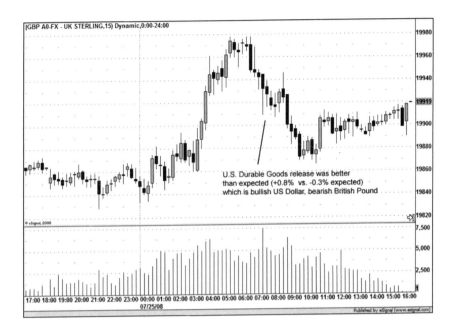

Figure 2-5 Better Than Expected U.S. Durable Goods Report Reinforces Current Trend

Figure 2-5 shows an example of a durable goods release that kept GBPUSD pointed lower. This is an example in which a market already had taken a direction and the report served to reinforce that existing bias.

Retail Sales

The monthly report on retail sales provides a reading on retail activity over the previous month that gives investors insight into consumer spending habits. The figures on retail sales are

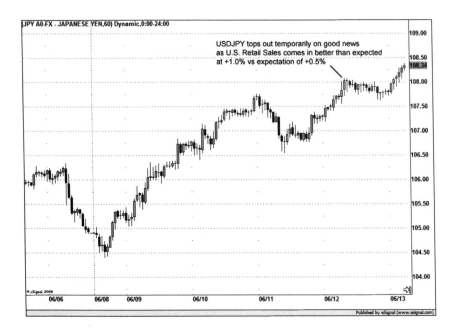

Figure 2-6 Traders Take Profit on Better Than Expected U.S. Retail Sales Release

released by the U.S. Census Bureau and can be found on its Web site at www.census.gov. Figure 2-6 shows a good example of a mature up move in a dollar-based pair. Traders took advantage of a dollar-friendly news release—a better than expected U.S. retail sales number—to exit their long positions, putting a temporary top in the market for that session.

Gross Domestic Product

The gross domestic product (GDP) is a measure of national income and output for the economy. It generally covers the previous quarter and then is annualized, and so it tends to be a

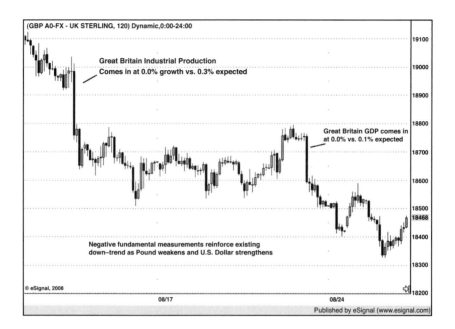

Figure 2-7 Fundamental Releases Support Existing Down Trend

lagging indicator. The textbook example for a recession is two straight quarters of negative GDP growth. We did not provide a graphic example for the U.S. GDP because the market rarely has a strong reaction to a U.S. GDP release, having taken its measurements and made its reactions from the more timely economic indicators. Figure 2-7 shows a chart for GBPUSD after a Great Britain GDP release that came in at zero growth and reinforced an existing downtrend.

The Producer Price Index

The producer price index (PPI) measures changes in the prices received by producers for their output. It is a key indicator in determining inflation on the production level. This number is reported by the U.S. Department of Labor, Bureau of Labor Statistics, at www.bls.gov. Generally, a higher than expected U.S. PPI release leads to U.S. dollar strength, as the expectation is that interest rates will be raised to combat inflation. Figure 2-8 shows an example of a slightly higher than expected PPI release, after which the U.S. dollar strengthens initially and the euro weakens. Once the selling dries up, the market still finds itself above the previous week's low price, and traders opt to take profits at the 146.50 level by buying back their short positions. This puts support in the market, and we see a rally going forward on what initially was taken as a bearish fundamental release for EURUSD.

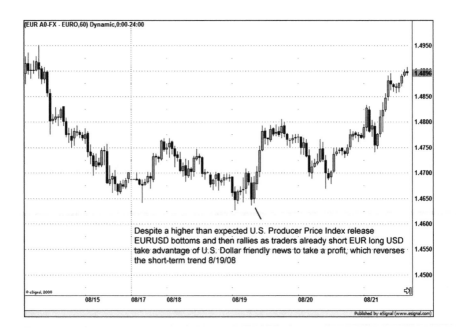

Figure 2-8 Despite Bearish News, EURUSD Reverses on Support after Dollar-Friendly News

The Consumer Price Index

The consumer price index (CPI) measures the average price of consumer goods and services bought by households. It is a key indicator in determining inflation on the retail level, as cost of living elements are factored into the prices. As with many other reports, there are multiple segments, but it is best to focus on the core rate and avoid being distracted by other segments. This number is reported by the U.S. Department of Labor, Bureau of Labor Statistics, at www.bls.gov.

A higher than expected CPI release generally leads to strength in the U.S. dollar. Figure 2-9 shows a USDCHF chart

U.S. Consumer Price Index comes in higher than expected and after initial reaction lower, USDCHF strengthens and rallies strongly on sentiment that U.S. Interest rates will have to rise to offset inflation

Figure 2-9 Initial Knee-Jerk Reaction Lower on Higher CPI Data Proves Short-Lived

in which there is a knee-jerk reaction lower to a CPI number that was higher than expected. However, once the price settles down and finds support around the previous session's low, the market turns and trades higher, in line with the higher than anticipated U.S. inflation numbers.

Consumer Confidence

The index of consumer confidence measures the level of economic optimism of consumers, based on their savings and spending activities; it generally is released on the last Tuesday of the month by The Conference Board at www.conference-board.org.

Figure 2-10 Higher Than Expected Consumer Confidence Data Support Existing Trend

As important as these reports and releases are, they are only lagging indicators as they generally provide the previous month's or quarter's activity. Generally, a higher than expected consumer confidence reading is read as positive for U.S. stocks and the U.S. dollar. Figure 2-10 shows a higher than expected consumer confidence reading, and the dollar trades higher as EURUSD falls sharply. The market was already in a pronounced downtrend, and the surprisingly stronger than expected U.S. confidence reading might have encouraged traders to add to their short positions or to exit long positions, which helped accelerate the down move already in place.

Leading Indicators

For leading indicators one looks to the markets themselves:

The S&P 500. This stock index consists of 500 of the top U.S. corporations. It provides a forward look on the health of some of the largest companies in the world and is thus a good gauge of the economy overall.

U.S. Treasury bonds and notes. These influential financial instruments provide a direct look at current and future interest rates as well as gauging demand for government securities.

U.S. dollar index. This currency index shows how the U.S. currency is faring relative to its trading partners' economies.

As an analyst or trader you need to do the following:

- Keep an economic calendar marked with the key release dates.
- Be aware of the major economic releases and the impact they can have.
- Stay abreast of major international developments and news as they affect the value of currency prices.
- Know that the currency markets of the major industrialized nations tend to be self-correcting price mechanisms. The very things that make a country's currency strong, such as a growing business environment and firming interest rates, in time will have the opposite effect as that demand will allow those countries' trading partners with cheaper currencies and lower interest rates to undercut their prices, leading to slower growth and lower interest rates in that country.
- If you are new to trading and economics, do not base trades solely on fundamentals at this point in your trading experience. The results are too unpredictable, and the risk too high. In general, however, fundamental analysis is most useful for long-term positions.

As you can see from the many examples just reviewed, there are times when the current trend in the market takes precedence over the fundamental news, just as there are times when a news release overrides the current trend. There are no constants in economic developments and releases because the economy and the many moving parts that constitute it constitute a very dynamic process. As traders, many of us devise a more accessible framework for determining the direction from which to trade a market not by studying the causes of price movement—the fundamentals—but by going along with the effects of price movement. You will never read the phrase *fundamentals versus technicals* in this book, as we know and understand the complementary value of both schools of thought.

Major Currencies

The U.S. dollar is still the most heavily traded global currency and has maintained its status as the world's reserve currency. Most central banks around the world maintain U.S. dollar reserves, and that adds to its influence, as do the fundamental news and data releases related to the U.S. economy, which is the world's largest. Because of this, the U.S. dollar, also known as the greenback, is a "flight to quality" currency; this was reaffirmed in mid-2008 when global stock markets came tumbling down and monies quickly flowed into dollars, creating a sharp and sustained rally for this currency. The global marketplace is a dynamic pricing apparatus that always is subject to change. However, at this time, the greenback is still the world's reserve currency. Because of this, all the other major currencies are quoted in relation to the U.S. dollar. The most influential factors in the pricing of the dollar come from the policies of the U.S. Federal Reserve, which is the central bank of the United States, and the U.S. Treasury.

The euro is the currency of the European Union and is second only to the U.S. dollar in terms of reserves held by other countries and central banks. Because of this, the EURUSD is the most heavily traded currency pair. The most influential factors in pricing the euro against other currencies are the policies of the European Central Bank. A consideration in understanding European Central Bank policies is that rather than speaking for one independent entity or country, it must balance the economic interests of many.

The Great Britain pound is arguably the oldest of the major currencies, with its issuer, the Bank of England, having been around since the 1600s. It is ranked third in currency reserves held around the world. GBPUSD is a heavily traded currency pair that in recent history has been a leader among the majors, having led the rally in 2006 and 2007 and having topped in 2008 and led the majors lower from there.

The Japanese yen is a very influential currency in that the Japanese economy is the second largest in the world and that nation's currency is the primary Asian representative in the forex markets. The central bank of Japan is the force behind the yen and is known for being more active than the other major central banks when it comes to managing the national currency.

The Canadian dollar is an influential currency because of the richness of that country's natural resources; the fact that it shares a border with the United States, the world's largest economy; and its European connections on its eastern coast and its Asian connections on its western coast. Canada is a truly 24-hour-a-day country.

The Australian dollar has become more and more influential over the last two decades as that country has become a major exporter of commodities to the growing Asian economies. Its location on the "global clock" also makes it an attractive currency for traders working the "third" shift: 4 p.m. to midnight Eastern Standard Time.

PART 3

TECHNICAL
ANALYSIS

CHAPTER 3

CHARTS FOR TRADING

For technical analysts, the art of trading starts with the chart. A chart is a sequence of prices plotted vertically over a horizontal time frame, with each individual price bar, or candle, marking the open, high, low, and last price for a particular time period: a week, a day, or an hour.

Charting and technical analysis overall are based on the assumption that actual price action is more significant than the information that has been reported to be the cause of that action. We assume that all known market information already has been deciphered by market participants and therefore is reflected in the last price. We don't doubt that fundamental information is often the driving force behind price action, but speaking for technicians, we know we will never have faster access to news and economic releases than the financial institutions with which we share the marketplace. If we can't compete with them in that regard, to be able to operate among them, we have to operate from a different vantage point, which technical analysis provides. This is not to say that price is always an accurate reflection of underlying value. On the basis of the positioning and emotions of market participants—that is, buyers and sellers—price fluctuates, sometimes greatly, from one day to the next. Technical analysis can provide a concise picture of those fluctuations and tell us who is controlling a market currently: the buyers or the sellers. The biggest advantage technical analysis has over fundamental analysis is that it takes much of the subjective nature out of the decision-making process.

As technicians we don't care about price outcome; that means we don't care if the market moves up or down. We are interested only in going where the market wants to take us. There is no opinion for us, no right or wrong price direction. We know it is unreasonable to think we can predict what will happen tomorrow, and so we always avoid getting attached to one outcome over another. We do not predict which way a market will move; we position ourselves to follow along with the market.

One of the first things the old-timers told us on the exchange floors was to "lose your opinion, not your money." Their point was that if you stay attached to your opinions and make decisions on that basis and on the emotions behind them, you'll probably lose money. That saying is one of the cornerstones of what we are going to teach you.

In analyzing markets, there are many choices in the tools we use, and choosing a chart is no different. In the charting package I use, seven different kinds of charts are listed. We will discuss the three most common ones now: line charts, bar charts, and candlestick charts.

Line Charts

Line charts show only the market's closing price and can be beneficial in that they smooth out the price action, making a trend or

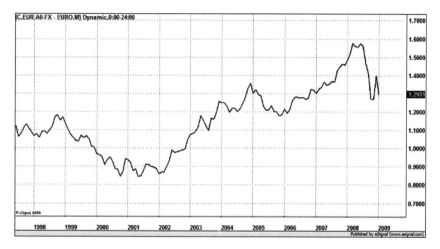

Figure 3-1   Line Chart

direction easier to discern. Figure 3-1 shows a monthly line chart for EURUSD.

The line chart is the most simple type of chart and can keep traders from overreacting to price extremes on a short-term basis. It also can make it easier to identify significant support and resistance levels and chart patterns, both of which we will be studying extensively in this book.

Bar Charts

Figure 3-2 shows a price bar from a bar chart. Bar charts show a market's open, high, low, and close on a vertical bar and therefore provide more information than does a line chart. On the left side of the bar a horizontal tab indicates the opening price for the time period, and on the right side a horizontal tab

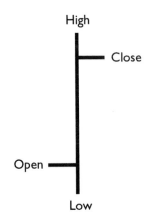

Figure 3-2 Price Bar

Figure 3-3 Monthly Bar Chart

indicates the closing price. The height of the bar represents the entire range of trading within that time frame; hence, it provides the high and the low.

Traditionally, bar charts were indicated in black and white, but newer programs use color designations such as green and red to indicate upward and downward movements in price.

Figure 3-3 shows a monthly bar chart.

In most charting packages the bars will be colored, with green bars indicating the months that closed higher than the previous month's close and red bars marking months that closed lower than the previous month's close. In Figure 3-3, notice the pattern of higher highs and higher lows before and then again after the price correction in 2005. This price behavior or pattern is characteristic of a bull market.

Candlestick Charts

Candlestick charts display basically the same information as bar charts but in a somewhat different way. Figure 3-4 shows that the "body" of the candle represents the difference between the open and the close. If the body is white (or green), the market moved up and the open is represented by the bottom edge. If the body is black (or red), the market moved down and the open is represented by the top edge. The shadows, which also are called wicks, are the lines above and below the candle body and represent the high and low of the time period. Figure 3-4 shows candles in black for a down candle and in white for an up candle.

Anatomy of a Candle

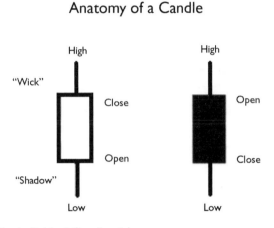

Figure 3-4 Individual Candlesticks

Bar Charts versus Candlestick Charts

Of the two chart types, many would argue that candlestick charts are the preferred type for trading. They give similar information when one is looking at a single time period, but more important, they visually signal other clues about the market when one is viewing a larger time frame. There are important things to note about the differences between bar charts and candlestick charts (see Figure 3-5):

- The color of the bar on the chart depends on the closing price of the previous bar. If the closing price of the current bar is higher than the closing price of the previous bar, the bar will be green (or white).
- The color of the candlestick depends only on the position of the close relative to the open for that time period.

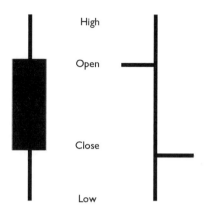

Candlestick versus Bar

Figure 3-5 Difference between a Candlestick and a Price Bar

- If the market closes higher than it opened, the candle will be green (or white).
- It's usually easier for beginners to work with candlestick charts.
- Candlesticks also provide the additional visual signals of trend shifts.

For examples of both types of charts in color go to www.Trading-U.com.

Candlestick Shapes: Body Size

One way candlesticks provide information about market behavior is through the length of the candle body. Figure 3-6 shows candles with long and short bodies. Long bodies indicate strong price movement, and short bodies tend to indicate indecision.

Long and Short Candle Bodies

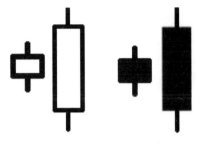

Figure 3-6 Different-Sized Candle Bodies Provide Information about Price Behavior

Long and Short Candle Shadows

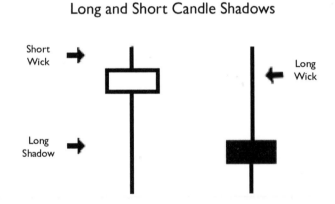

Figure 3-7 Long Shadows Yield Further Insight into Price Behavior

Another way candlesticks provide information about market behavior is through the length of the shadows or wicks. Long shadows represent a failed attempt to move a market in that direction (see Figure 3-7).

Candlestick Shapes: Doji

The doji (Figure 3-8) represents indecision regarding price and frequently occurs near market highs or market lows. It is characterized by a body that is very small and usually has long wicks. We will talk more later in this chapter about how to use the doji as a signal of a change in market direction.

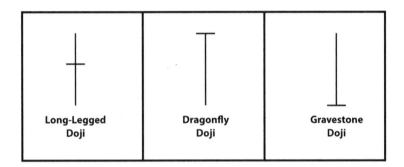

Long-Legged Doji   **Dragonfly Doji**   **Gravestone Doji**

Figure 3-8   Different Types of Dojis

Spinning Tops

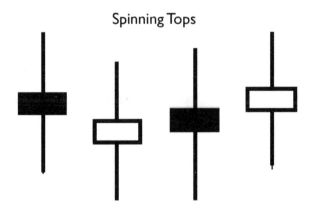

Figure 3-9   Spinning Tops Are Similar to Dojis

Candlestick Shapes: Spinning Tops

Spinning tops (Figure 3-9) are similar to dojis in that they have short bodies and long wicks, with both indicating indecision in the market. They can occur at market tops or bottoms, but they also can show up in sideways-moving markets and during periods of low volume.

Bullish Candle Formations

Some of the most useful information can be gained from candlesticks when they signal a change of direction in the market. Figure 3-10 shows six common formations that may indicate that the market is headed upward.

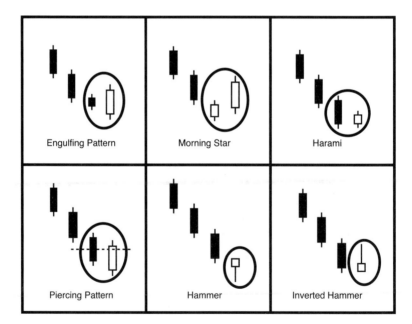

Figure 3-10 Potentially Bullish Candle Patterns

Bearish Candle Formations

Figure 3-11 shows potentially bearish candlestick patterns.

Figure 3-12 shows a daily EURUSD candlestick chart.

An important aspect of price charts, whether bar charts, candlestick charts, or line charts, is that they provide a historical perspective on a market's previous behavior. We can't overstress the importance of having enough information or time on your charts when you are analyzing a market that you potentially will trade. If you were going to hire a person to work closely with you, you would want to know more about that person than what her last job was. You would want an accurate picture of her entire work history before you made that commitment. You probably would not want to waste time asking questions to see

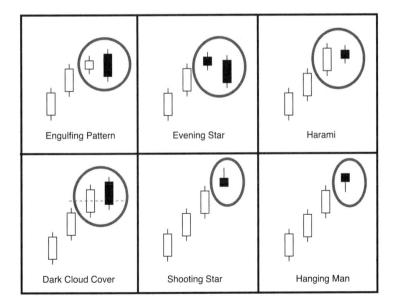

Figure 3-11   Potentially Bearish Candlestick Patterns

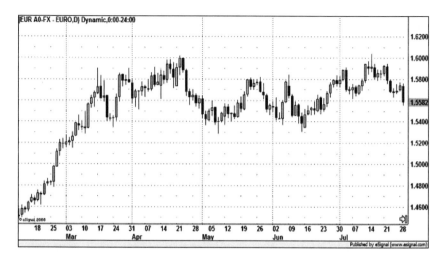

Figure 3-12   Daily Candlestick Chart

if she was qualified for the job at hand until you had enough of a work history to give you some insight into her likely future behavior. Similarly, we always start out analyzing a chart by going back as far as we can to get a broad view of its long-term behavior. As you get closer to a trading decision, it is okay to home in and see specific candle behavior, but to start we want to know how this market behaved historically.

CANDLESTICK CHARTS

Higher Time Frame Charts First

To gain the historical perpective needed to analyze markets, we always start from the highest time frame chart. Figure 4-1 shows a monthly chart that supplies a fairly clear picture of the levels that bound the USDJPY market from 1997 to 2008. Many inexperienced traders make the mistake of thinking that a chart with such a high time frame is not needed, particularly if they are using charts with lower time frames. In our work we could not disagree more. Any signal generated by a monthly chart is significant.

We look at the long view first to get the big picture. On the basis of where the market shown in Figure 4-1 has traded over this long-term period, we can surmise that it's not unreasonable to see large, sustained price movements. This

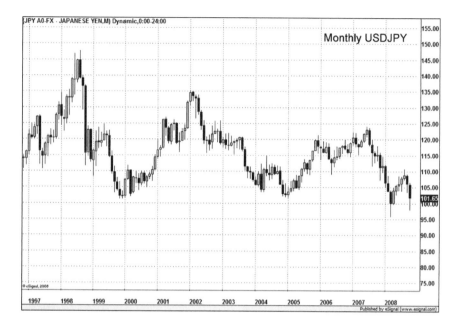

Figure 4-1 Monthly USDJPY Chart

market, which is USDJPY, could continue to provide us with good trading opportunities. We see a pattern of lower highs over this period and a habit of finding support plus or minus 2.5 or so points of 100.00 over those years. The next step would be to take a look at the chart of the next lower time frame, which would be the weekly chart:

The weekly chart in Figure 4-2 provides a picture of how this market has traded over the years from 2004 to 2008. We can see that this market is in the lower half of its six-year range and is showing a pattern of lower lows over the last five years. Here we are still just looking at the big picture, not focusing on individual candles.

Figure 4-2 Weekly USDJPY Chart

To get a more updated view of this market, we drop down to a daily chart.

On the daily chart in Figure 4-3 we see that this market is in a three-month downtrend, which is in line with the overall downtrend in the higher time frames, as defined by the pattern of lower highs and lower lows over the last year.

Thus, by glancing at these three charts—the monthly, the weekly, and the daily—we've brought ourselves up to historical speed with this market. At this point we can hone in to take a closer look at what the candles are telling us on a shorter-term basis, within the context of the long-term picture.

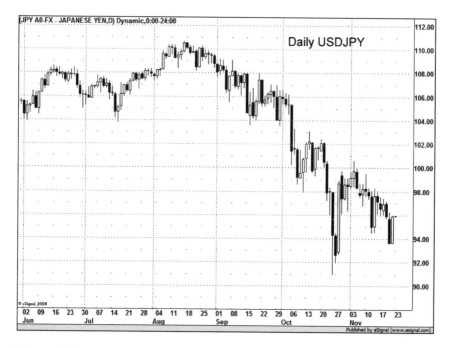

JPY A0-FX - JAPANESE YEN,D) Dynamic,0:00-24:00

Daily USDJPY

Figure 4-3 USDJPY Daily Chart

Trending and Countertrending Markets

The individual candle indicates the market's path of least resistance for that period. When a candle has a long body, it is telling us that the move has conviction; in other words, it is an impulsive move. Conversely, when the candle has a small body, it is telling us that the move for this period is lacking in conviction and probably is characterized by reactive behavior. The distinction between impulsive and reactive behavior, taken collectively, is how we recognize whether a market is exhibiting trending or countertrending behavior. This is an important aspect of market

66

behavior to recognize. When we see that a market has strong conviction, or momentum, by noting how long the rectangular body of the candle is, we need to recognize that the market is showing us its current trend. When we see sideways price action, or ranging behavior, and candles with small bodies, we know we are in a market trading counter to the trend, and we don't expect extended moves until we see a clear breach of that range. This distinction between trending behavior and countertrending behavior can be seen clearly in Figure 4-4.

The two different types of price behavior shown in Figure 4-4 represent an important distinction that can provide insight into

Figure 4-4   Trending and Countertrending Price Action

a market's future direction. There are actually two types of impulsive or trending behavior to account for: one going with the long-term or primary trend and the second marking the beginning of an intermediate-term trend that also is known as a secondary move. We will cover the subject of coordinating time frames in detail in Chapter 9 in the section on quantifying trends.

Watching the Clock

The most important thing we need to know about an individual candle is that we do not make an analytic, or trading, decision until the candle is closed, which means that the time period is complete. You will be hearing this again. Another important aspect of individual candle analysis for forex intraday charts is the time of day. In trading, even for the 24-hour-a-day market, all time periods are not equal. If there is very little trading volume, as is generally the case from the close of the U.S. financial markets through the Tokyo open, we do not place importance on individual candles or patterns during this period. In forex markets, it is widely known by experienced traders that volume generally trails off noticeably leading up to noon EST and stays very low until the Tokyo open. Regardless of your own experience in trading, you do not want to initiate short-term trades that are based on individual candles or candle formations during those hours. The exception to this would be U.S. stock indexes such as the E-mini S&P future and the mini Dow futures contract, which still have high volume and good trader participation rates. In Chapter 11 we will cover trading for different periods and define position trading, swing trading, and day trading.

Individual Candles Can Exhibit Noteworthy Behavior

The first two types of candles we want to point out to start are dojis, which are candles in which the opening price is very close to the closing price and there is a very small body; these candles indicate market indecision. Change-of-direction candles tend to reverse the previous pattern or direction of the highs and lows. If the preceding candles were moving higher, a change-of-direction candle would be a candle in which the close was lower than the low of the preceding candle or candles. Similarly, if the previous candles had developed a pattern of lower lows, lower highs, or lower closes, a change-of-direction candle would be a candle that closed above the high of the previous candle or candles. Figure 4-5 is a daily chart of the British pound from January 20, 2007 that exhibits its share of both dojis and change-of-direction candles.

You will learn in Chapter 9 that change-of-direction candles are used as trade signals. It is important that as analysts and traders we understand that neither one of these candles means that a market will or will not perform as we expect. Change-of-direction candles do not mean the market is going to change direction, just as a doji does not mean the market must take a breather or must reverse. We never know what event could happen at any time to change the behavior of the market. Over time, though, these candles have proved to be a good hint or heads-up that a particular market has shifted gears, and it's important that you file this information away as you will see how we use it to home in on specific trade setups. Notice in Figure 4-5 how twice we see a doji candle followed by the

Dojis and Change-of-Direction Candles

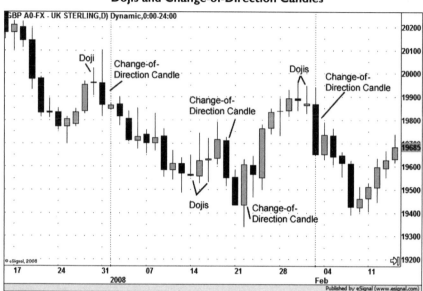

Figure 4-5 Dojis and Change-of-Direction Candles

change-of-direction candle to put in a market top. This is indecision followed by action as the British pound completes an up move before swinging lower.

It's important to recognize what behavior the candles or multicandle formations are exhibiting in the context of the overall trends that already are in place. Taken by themselves, dojis or any individual candle or candle formations may or may not be significant. However, in the context of the current trends and relative to significant support and resistance, they are worth our attention as traders and, as you will see later, play a significant role in helping identify trade setups and signals.

In Chapter 3 we talked about some of the major candlestick formations. Some of those formations (see Figure 4-6), which can include dojis (depending on the size of the reversal candle bodies), are *shooting stars,* which also are referred to as evening doji stars, and *hammers,* which may be referred to as hammer dojis. A candle we did not mention is the *inside candle,* which can be either a reversal or a continuation signal. An inside candle is essentially a candle that is engulfed by the previous candle. If the market reverses after an inside candle, the engulfed candle will go on to become a harami pattern; if that does not happen, it will become a continuation pattern. What

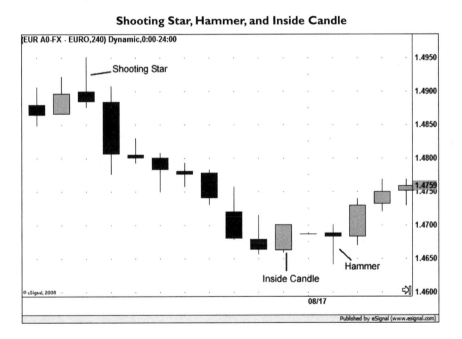

Figure 4-6   Shooting Star, Inside Candle, and Hammer

is significant about the inside candle is whether the market closes above or below it, as price has a tendency to continue in that direction.

Figure 4-6 is a 240-minute chart of EURUSD with a shooting star doji in the upper left corner of the chart before a move lower, then an inside bar toward the bottom of the chart with the market stabilizing, and then a hammer doji, followed by a change-of-direction candle before an up move.

The inside candle is telling us that the market lacks conviction in regard to its direction. The inside candle is considered pivotal in that the market is expected to increase momentum in whichever direction it closes in relation to the high and low of the inside candle. A close above the high of the inside candle is considered bullish, and a close below the low of that candle is considered bearish. When you are viewing intraday forex charts, keep in mind that low-volume candles such as those between 17:00 and midnight Greenwich Mean Time (GMT) should be discounted, as their behavior is not considered nearly as significant as that of candles on higher volume. The hammer, which is also a doji, is considered a bullish candle. A hammer is created after the market trades lower after the opening before moving higher and closing in the top third of the range. What has happened is that price probed lower during that period but found support as buying came into the market to propel it higher. The long shadow stands as evidence that lower prices were rejected. When it is seen in a downtrend, this behavior can be taken as indicative that the market is pausing or possibly trying to reverse. The shooting star is also a doji and is similar to the hammer but is considered a bearish candle. When it comes after a rally or uptrend, it indicates that the market could be ready for a pause or a reversal. The long wick and short body below it in Figure 4-6 emphasize that the higher prices were rejected.

Always remember that individual candles and candle formations do not necessarily predict what a market will do; that is, they do not always work out in favor of our position. There is always a danger in looking at a short-term indication such as an individual candle that we may be missing something of importance in the big picture. Candle patterns play an important part in our analysis and trading and are especially useful when combined with other aspects of technical analysis. We should never take a trade solely on the basis of an individual candle or bar or even chart pattern without considering additional factors, such as whether this price behavior came on support or resistance.

For forex markets, we discount candles and formations during low-volume, low-trade periods such as from lunchtime in New York to the Tokyo open, and we do not make any analytic or trading decisions until the candle is closed. You will find that knowing that you do not have to make a trading decision until the candle closes will keep you relaxed, as you know there is no action to take until a specific time.

Two candle formations that often signal a market pause or reversal are the bullish engulfing pattern and the bearish engulfing pattern. Both also can be change-of-direction candles, depending on their close in proximity to the previous candle's high or low. Another candle that can be either one of these is a *benchmark candle*, which we will cover shortly.

A bullish engulfing pattern occurs when a green (white) candle's body surrounds or engulfs and then closes above the previous candle's red (black) body. A bearish engulfing pattern occurs when a red (black) candle's body surrounds or engulfs and then closes below the previous candle's green (white) body. It is this close above the previous candle's high or below the previous candle's low that makes engulfing candles change-of-direction candles.

In Figure 4-7, in the middle of the chart, we see two hammer dojis, with the second hammer followed by a bullish engulfing candle. We see that the body of that hammer is surrounded by the body of the engulfing candle and that the engulfing candle closes above the high of the preceding candle.

Bullish Engulfing Pattern

Figure 4-7 Hammers and Bullish Engulfing Candle

Bearish Engulfing Pattern

Figure 4-8 Shooting Star Followed by Bearish Engulfing Pattern

Figure 4-8 shows a shooting star doji that marks a top in EURUSD on a 240-minute chart at approximately 160.00, followed by a bearish engulfing candle that precludes a major sell-off in the market. Note also the number of dojis and inside candles on the right. That spells indecision on behalf of influential players or traders in this market.

A benchmark candle (see Figure 4-9) is an elongated engulfing candle with few or no wicks and leaves no doubt about who won out at the end of the candle, the bulls or the bears. The term *benchmark candle* came from the trader and author John L. Person, president of www.nationalfutures.com. What we will learn to appreciate about markets is that they have a tendency to pull back in the opposite direction after a bench-mark candle to retest the previous conviction. A rule of thumb is that if we see a retracement after a benchmark candle, we should look for it to stop halfway into the candle, giving us a 50 percent retracement, before resuming the direction set by the benchmark. We will study a market's tendency to retrace further in the section on Fibonacci retracements and extensions in the material on support and resistance in Chapter 5.

Figure 4-9 shows a classic example of a benchmark candle in EURJPY on a 15-minute chart; this candle is also a bearish engulfing candle or a change-of-direction candle. A benchmark

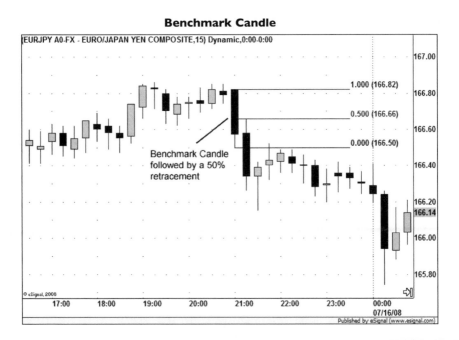

Figure 4-9 Benchmark Candle Followed by 50 Percent Retracement

candle is a long candle with few or no wicks and leaves no doubt about the direction of the market. In this case the market sold off hard to close below the lows of the last eight candles, very likely clearing out plenty of long positions along the way. There is no doubt that this is bearish behavior. Before the down move accelerated, however, note how the market went back and retraced 50 percent of the benchmark candle. The fact that benchmark candles have a tendency to do that is good information to have, because it will give you a chance to get in on the move or exit a position if a benchmark traps you while you are going the wrong way.

We have seen how the longer-term charts give us historical perspective on price direction and behavior and how individual candles and candle formations provide a good look at current price action and can help us in timing trades. Now let's tie the two together and study how shorter-term or intraday charts can show us market behavior for a specific period within the context of the long-term trend. This is important information to have because just as people develop patterns or habits that we want to know about before interacting with them, so do markets. It is through recognizing these characteristics that we are able to measure a market's current direction and know what price action or behavior to look for to tell us that the direction is pausing or changing.

Figure 4-10 is a 240-minute chart of the mini Dow futures contract. We can see from glancing at the chart that through the second half of June and the first half of July this market was in an obvious downtrend. Note the pattern of lower lows and lower highs. This happens to be an impulse down move in a bear market, and so it is to be expected that by using bearish

Figure 4-10   Series of Bearish Change-of-Direction Candles

change-of-direction candles or bearish engulfing patterns to enter short trades, a trader will find himself or herself on the right side of the trend. Now take a look at the right side of the chart and you will see how the market broke the previous cycle of lower lows by posting a couple of bullish change-of-direction candles in mid-July, followed by a higher high. The fact that a higher high on a closing basis followed the bullish change-of-direction candles was a signal to exit any short trades.

In Figure 4-11 we take a closer look at the same mini Dow futures contract as it starts to bottom out in mid-July 2008. Note that there is a failed bearish engulfing pattern on July 10. That is a hint that perhaps the power of the sell-off is waning. We do get a shooting star doji, which is a topping candle, afterward, followed by a sell-off through the London

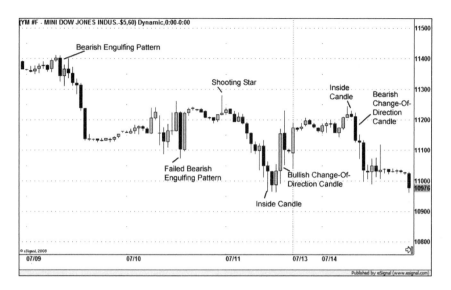

Figure 4-11 Collective Candle Behavior before Market Reversal

session and the U.S. a.m. session. Just ahead of lunch on July 11, which is a Friday, we see a hammer and then an inside bar, followed two candles later by a sharp change-of-direction candle higher ahead of the weekend as longer-term, higher time frame traders take profits ahead of the weekend. The following Monday, July 14, 2008, it's back to business as the market gives us a shooting star followed by an inside candle and then a bearish change-of-direction candle that does not look back. The 11,000 level did hold as the market reversed and launched a short-covering rally that carried the Dow to 11,800 by mid-August.

Figure 4-12 shows a 15-minute USDJPY chart in which a bearish change-of-direction candle an hour after the London open sets the day's tone with an obvious pattern of lower lows

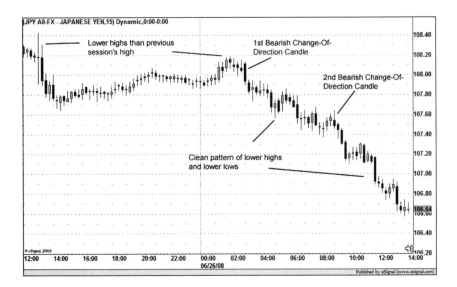

Figure 4-12 Bearish Change-of-Direction Candles Followed by Lower Highs and Lows

and lower highs, followed by a second bearish change-of-direction an hour after the U.S. open that accelerates the sell-off.

Over the course of this chapter you have seen how the collective behavior of the individual candles establishes and reinforces the direction for the trends on the charts for all time frames. It is often said in this business that one day does not make a trend, but one candle can shift a trend, another can reinforce that shift, and a third can confirm that shift. The study of individual candles and candlestick formations in all time frames is an important aspect of trading and is well worth the time it takes to review their behavior on a regular basis.

CHAPTER 5

SUPPORT AND RESISTANCE

The next aspect of charting a trader needs to understand is support and resistance. Markets generally move up and down in a somewhat irregular manner and rarely reach the point to which they are heading in a straight line. A bull market moves up and then generally pulls back slightly and finds support before continuing to climb higher. A bear market moves lower and then pauses and tries to move up before running into resistance and turning lower again. A resistance level is defined as a point at which the market has stopped and moved lower; conversely, a support level is a point at which the market has stopped and bounced higher. An example of support and resistance levels in EURJPY is shown in Figure 5-1.

Defined another way, support is a price level at which there is strong demand; buyers step up and purchase a market aggressively, in bulk. Conversely, resistance is a level at which supply is abundant and buyers are scarce; competing sellers

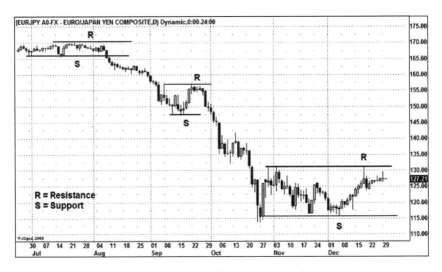

Figure 5-1 Horizontal Support and Resistance Levels

mark down price quickly to entice the shrinking pool of buyers. Typically, whenever we see an isolated high point or low point on a chart, we know that it is at that point that demand overpowered supply or supply overwhelmed demand. Support and resistance levels are drawn horizontally on the chart and mark isolated high and low points.

As a market reaches a level of support or resistance, it often will "test" that level, as can be seen in Figure 5-2. The level may hold, or the market may move right through it. For this reason, we say that support and resistance levels are estimated; we have no guarantee that they will hold under live market conditions. A market is said to have broken a level of resistance or support if a candle closes beyond that level. This is what makes the closing price of a candle so important. In Figure 5-2 the market

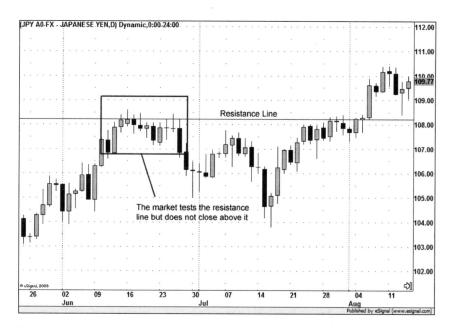

Figure 5-2   Importance of Waiting for a Close above Resistance

flirted with the 108.25 level in June and then again in late July before finally closing above it in early August 2008.

Trendlines

One of the tenets of technical analysis is that prices trend. Trendlines are made by connecting two or more points of support or resistance. Those lines can trend up, down, or sideways, but once a direction is established, it tends to become self-fulfilling. A downtrend means a series of price bars or candles exhibiting lower highs, lower lows, and lower closes;

conversely, an uptrend means higher lows, higher highs, and higher closes. One way to define a trend is by drawing trendlines, as shown in Figures 5-3 and 5-4. We draw support or up trendlines by drawing a straight line connecting the higher lows and extending it into the future. We draw resistance or down trendlines by drawing a straight line connecting the lower highs and extending it into the future. In trading, it is the market that defines our decisions, or parameters, and it is trendlines that define the market's parameters. Trendlines are a favorite tool among traders for a very good reason: Markets respect them. Uptrends, or bull trendlines, act as areas of support. Downtrends, or bear trendlines, act as levels of resistance. Trendlines have to be updated as the market moves through time, and they can be used for

Figure 5-3 Support Line Connecting Isolated Lows

Figure 5-4 Resistance Lines Connecting Isolated Highs

both trading and forecasting. In drawing trendlines on candlestick charts, we also have the option of drawing them from the highs and lows of the wicks or from the highs and lows of the bodies.

Figure 5-5 shows a monthly chart of GBPUSD with all significant support and resistance levels and trendlines marked. Note how in the summer of 2008 the support level that had built up through the first half of that year gave way. It is essential that a trader monitor significant levels like this and be aware of the possible market consequences for price when a major level is breached and price closes beyond it. This price breakdown was followed by penetration of the long-term bull trendline, and a major sell-off followed.

Figure 5-5 Support and Resistance Levels on a Monthly Chart

In this figure we can see from the pattern of higher highs and higher lows from 2002 through 2007 that the trend is higher. We also can see that just above the 210.00 level, supply started to exceed demand and buying disappeared as sellers offered aggressively lower prices. Conversely, when prices went below 194.00 in early 2008, demand picked up and buyers provided support multiple times at this level. We also see a sideways pattern of successive dojis that spells price indecision for the first seven months of 2008.

Next, we examine a weekly chart of the same market extending back a little more than two years.

In Figure 5-6 we get a closer look at the correction or resting period GBPUSD was in through the first half of 2008.

Regardless of this back-and-forth price action, by keeping those trendlines drawn from the monthly chart in place, we don't lose sight of the long-term trend. There are always two sides to a market, and we are reminded of this as supply above the market shows its hand in March 2008 and rejects the market's attempts to rise above 204.00. Once again demand dries up on the rally as buyers drop their bids and sellers move prices down quickly to unload inventory. Once prices pull back in May and again in June, we see the importance of the horizontal support level drawn from the January lows. It becomes clear that we are in a long-term uptrend and that buying support is rewarded as the British pound continues to have demand at the 194.00 level. As is always the case

Figure 5-6   Support and Resistance Levels on a Weekly Chart

in trading, this information is twofold as the bounces off 194.00 tell us there is support in place and at the same time tell us that a close below that level would be a strong indication of market weakness or even a possible market reversal, which is what did happen.

Figure 5-7 shows a weekly chart of the U.S. stock market as represented by the S&P 500 stock index futures, in which a break of the long-term trendline in late 2007–early 2008 marked a key reversal of the previous 4.5-year bull market.

The events might be easier to see now, but amid the emotions of making a trading decision, all too often the student forgets about the long-term trend in the face of a fluctuating account balance. The more experience you gain as a trader, the more respect you will develop for the long-term trend. Respecting

Figure 5-7 Support Line Gives Way on a Weekly U.S. Stock Market Chart

88

long-term trendlines is a twofold process: You respect them when they hold up and recognize that a big move may be in the making when they do not hold up and the market settles through them. As you can see from the chart in Figure 5-7, charts and trendlines are not just for traders. Investors would have been served well by exitinged long-term stock holdings on the basis of the stock market's trend reversal at the beginning of 2008.

Short-Term, Intermediate-Term, and Long-Term Trendlines

In doing trendline analysis, we need to understand that just as there are long-term, intermediate-term, and short-term trends

Figure 5-8   Long-Term, Intermediate-Term, and Short-Term Trendlines

simultaneously unfolding in a market, there are long-term, intermediate-term, and short-term trendlines. This is the case because as a trend extends itself, its angle, or slope, may increase or decrease as the market adjusts to the supply available for sale and the demand from buyers. To keep up with these ebbs and flows in price action, we must update our trendlines continuously, as illustrated in Figure 5-8.

Market Corrections

In Figure 5-8, a USDCHF 240-minute chart, we see the long-term trendline, then the intermediate-term trendline, and then the short-term trendline. This is a good example of how markets trend and serves as a reminder of why we need to keep trendlines updated. It also shows another aspect of trendlines, which is that not only do they serve as support or resistance, they also serve as attractors. Note what happens when the angle, or slope, between price and the trendline becomes steeper as the market moves lower. Similar to a mean reverting mechanism, the farther the slope increases, the more likely it becomes that price will react back toward the trendline. The slope can act as a rubber band that when stretched too far snaps back, taking the price the other way. These snapbacks, or retracements, are to be expected. "Expect corrections" is essential advice for traders. Once price does rally back on the USDCHF 240-minute chart, then falters, and then resumes the previous long-term downtrend or resumes its path of least resistance, we draw a new trendline. The process of price motion based on supply, demand, and the emotions of market participants plays out again in a cycle of lower highs and lower lows until eventually it shifts to a pattern of higher lows and then higher highs.

The daily chart in Figure 5-9 shows another example of a market that corrects only after sharp sell-offs, leaving us to update the new bear trendlines it creates.

Notice how every time the market increases its speed, angles away from the oldest or longest trendline, and goes vertical on the chart, it sets itself up to give us a snapback correction, or a countertrend rally back toward the older or longer-term trendline. Experienced traders tend to trade larger positions, and so it is their "covering," or buying back shares or contracts after the accelerated sell-offs, that starts the countertrend process.

Figure 5-9 Price Corrections after Trendline Violations

Once the market makes a countertrend move and then reverts lower, we draw a new, shorter-term trendline. These newer trendlines are going to help us understand the when of the next price correction. When we see price angling away from the new trendline as it accelerates, we should understand that in terms of time, that market is getting closer to a countertrend correction. Think of a correction as a car traveling at a high speed that needs to slow down before making a turn. A similar dynamic is at work with markets, and the trendlines generally tell us when that resting point occurs or where that turn is. More specifically, they give us a heads-up about when an impulsive, or trending, market will revert to a reactive, or countertrending, stance. Another way of putting this is that once a market has reached a point at which its momentum is exhausted, it's time for a correction. The trendlines on the daily USDJPY chart in Figure 5-9 provide that point. Each new trendline becomes steeper, leading us closer to the correction. For traders, it's difficult and unnecessary to calculate exactly when the correction will come; we just need to monitor the market when we see the slope of the trend increasing and exit a portion of our position once we get a close above (or below) the steepest or shortest-term trendline, being mindful that price has a tendency to migrate back to its longer-term trendlines.

By using the EURUSD 60-minute chart shown in Figure 5-10, we can take a closer look at price behavior by marking the previous daily lows and highs. We've also connected the isolated highs on the left side of the chart with a bear trendline and connected the isolated lows on the right side with a bull trendline. By marking both the previous highs and lows and the isolated highs and lows used to draw the trendlines, we generate

Figure 5-10 Daily Highs and Lows and Trendlines Help Distinguish Directional Shifts

a simple visual that shows when this market shifted from lower highs and lower lows to higher lows and higher highs. This illustration makes the point that although the trendlines are important, it is the previous highs and lows that we take as the measurements and draw the lines from that help us determine direction. Marking these previous highs and lows is also a valuable habit when it comes to operating in markets in which an uptrend or downtrend is not so clear.

The tendency of price to increase the slope of its path of least resistance over time, which we talked about before, and the tendency of that behavior to hasten corrections also can help alert us to the possibility of snapback moves or countertrend price behavior.

Figure 5-11 shows how horizontal support and resistance levels create a sideways channel. We know that support and resistance levels mark key price levels at which either the buyers or the sellers were proved right decisively. A support level marks a clear-cut level below where the market is trading where demand, or buying, absorbed the selling pressure through more aggressive bidding. It can be said that demand at that level was strong enough to prevent lower prices. Resistance, in contrast, is a clear-cut level above the market where supply, or sellers, intimidated buyers into backing off to establish dominance. It can be said that supply at that point overwhelmed demand and that prices at that higher level were

Sideways Channei

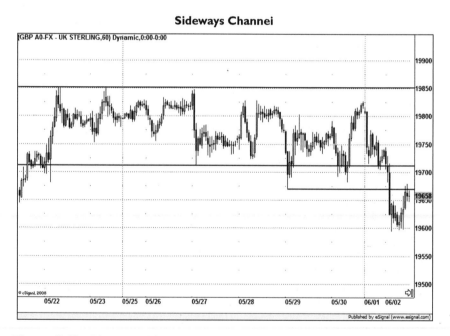

Figure 5-11 Horizontal Support and Resistance Create a Sideways Channel

94

unsustainable. We will cover price channels in Chapter 6 in the section on price formations, but we can see now how it's actually support and resistance levels and the trendlines drawn from them that are the basis for chart formation.

Figure 5-12 shows a commonly seen situation. More often than not a trading range proves to be a price pause before resumption in the same direction in which the market was moving before entering the range. This occurs because markets tend to trend more than they reverse.

Trendlines can be horizontal or angular and connect to at least two price points, with the third point adding validity. This is a

Resuming the Trend after a Pause

Figure 5-12 Horizontal Trading Range Provides a Pause before Continuation in the Same Direction

Figure 5-13 Third Point Confirms a Trendline

very important concept because it is at these "third points" on the trendline that one often sees a confluence of other support or resistance levels in the form of previous highs and lows, pivot points, and retracements, which we'll discuss later in this chapter. These confluences, or crossroads, of support will help us highlight trade signals that we might not be homed in on if we waited for the longer-term trendlines. Figure 5-13 shows that on May 1 the trendline intersected with the previous day's low. This may not look that significant at first glance on the daily chart, but for an intraday trader it proved to be a big move.

Another principle of technical analysis is that resistance can turn into support levels and vice versa. Figure 5-14

Figure 5-14 Resistance Lines Turn into Support Levels

shows a pair of trendlines that gave way; they did not hold as resistance but remained in place and gave us support on the retest. This highlights why we always have to update our trendlines and also leave the trendlines in place as they will aid us in spotting trend reversals, which often are marked by support turning into resistance and vice versa.

It is very important to see how price reacts to support and resistance levels before acting on them. We do this by waiting for an individual candle to close and then updating our trendlines if necessary before committing to a direction or trade, as shown in Figure 5-15. We do this to let the market gauge the strength or weakness of the support or resistance level. We always trade from the perspective that we do not know whether the level will hold. We do not try to guess whether the level will hold; we stay patient and let the market tell us if it is respecting the potential support or resistance. Remember to "lose your opinion, not your money." Once the candle is closed, we get a true snapshot of its behavior. For example, if price stalls at a particular level and then briefly probes below it before retreating, that is very different from what happens when it moves right through that level and closes beyond it. Figure 5-15 shows that price moved above the first trendline before pulling back. This prompted us to update our trendline and watch as the market made another move down before turning up on May 22, 2008. This is why it is so important to

Figure 5-15 Wait for Candle to Close above the Trendline

wait for the close of the candle before entering a trade. As technical analysts we must be as flexible as the markets we trade.

Trendlines are very useful for pointing out direction. Price doesn't have to go up to the trendline and give us a textbook trigger every time. In many cases just having the trendline in place on the chart will provide a reminder of a market's current direction. This is going to prove to be valuable information once you gain a little experience at demo trading and start to see firsthand how trending markets move *a lot* faster than do countertrending markets. You may have an extra minute or two to analyze a countertrend trigger, but with a trend trigger, you are not going to have that extra blink to think about it; if you wait, you will miss the bus.

The USDCHF 60-minute chart in Figure 5-16 provides a good example of a buy signal in an uptrend in which if we had waited for the market to give us a trendline test, we would have missed out on a nice trade. We use trendlines to remind us of the overall direction of the trend just as much as we use them to show support or resistance. It is very important to have your trendlines in place on the chart before starting to trade because if you are trading on a short-term basis, you need to concentrate on execution, not analysis. With your support levels in place, there is no thinking or questioning whether you are trading with the trend or counter to it. The difference lies in whether you observe it more loosely and let the profit run—trend trade—or take a profit or loss quickly, depending on short-term price behavior such as candlestick formations and current structure charts (support and resistance); that is, countertrend trading depends on the current long-term and short-term trendlines.

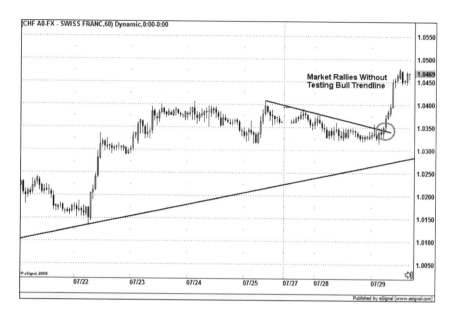

Figure 5-16 Existing Long-Term Trendlines Provide Direction

Pivot Points

We have looked at trendlines and the way they provide support and resistance, which we now know is what defines a market's parameters. We know that just as there are long-term trends and short-term trends, there are trendlines on different time frames. Now we need to cover another very influential form of support and resistance, one that also can be measured on different time frames: pivot points.

Pivot points are a popular and useful trader's tool. Jay Norris was introduced to them on the floor of the Chicago Board of Trade many years ago, when they were used primarily by professional traders. Pivot points are a simple rough-and-ready calculation that is used to determine underlying strength and weakness and provide potential support and resistance levels for a specific period. They are always calculated from the previous period's high, low, and close. Here is the formula for the different levels:

$$Resistance\ 3\ = high + 2 * (pivot - low)$$
$$Resistance\ 2\ = pivot + (R1 - S1)$$
$$Resistance\ 1\ = (2 * pivot) - low$$
$$Central\ pivot\ point\ = (high + close + low)/3$$
$$Support\ 1\ = (2 * pivot) - high$$
$$Support\ 2\ = pivot - (R1 - S1)$$
$$Support\ 3\ = low - 2 * (high - pivot)$$

Most charting packages will calculate these numbers for you, but it's important to understand the math behind the number.

Figure 5-17 shows a 240-minute EURUSD chart with the weekly pivots displayed.

For charts that are less than 60 minutes we use daily pivots, which are calculated from the previous daily range's high, low, and close; for charts 60 minutes or more we use the weekly pivots, which are calculated from the previous week's high, low, and close; and for daily charts, we use the monthly pivots, which are based on the previous month's high, low, and close. We also can calculate quarterly, yearly, presidential cycle, and even decade pivots. Many professional traders follow the shorter-term pivots, and that is why they tend to work so well: The levels are self-fulfilling because influential traders key off them. We view the central pivot point as support or resistance, depending on the side price opens and

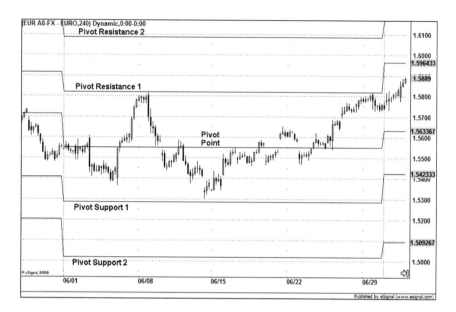

Figure 5-17 Weekly Pivot Points on a 240-Minute Chart

then trades on. Price below the central pivot can be seen as market weakness; similarly, price above the central pivot can be viewed as market strength. Pivot levels can work particularly well when there are no scheduled news releases or unexpected fundamental developments, leaving the market to bracket back and forth between the pivots. In a flat or sideways environment the market will tend to wrap around its central pivot, using pivot support 1 (S1) for support and pivot resistance 1 (R1) for resistance. In an uptrend price often tends to respect the central pivot or S1 as support and R2 as resistance, whereas in a downtrend price tends to respect the central pivot or R1 as resistance and S2 as support. Pivots points, like trendlines, are potential support and resistance levels. Therefore, we do not guess whether they will hold; we observe the market's behavior in relation to them.

The daily GBPUSD chart in Figure 5-18 shows monthly pivots. Note the difference from the previous example in that the pivots change monthly. Clearly, the GBPUSD has a strong tendency to respect its monthly pivots, as we see how the central pivot provided resistance in February before providing support in March. Then we see the central pivot again provide resistance in April and again in late May, whereas S2 provides support in May and S1 provides support in June. Note also that in nearly every month on the chart the central pivot played a key role in helping us gauge underlying strength and weakness. The trading for this particular period can be called

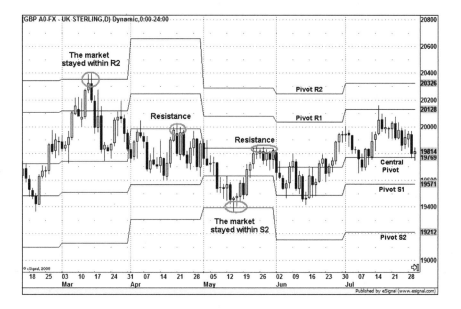

Figure 5-18 Monthly Pivot Points on a Daily GBPUSD Chart

countertrending. We can see the sideways back-and-forth action, which technically shows up as the market generally staying within S1 and R1.

This example highlights the fact that pivots adjust from one month to the next. This is a characteristic that is conducive to both trend trading and countertrend trading. The farther the market travels in one direction in one month, the more the pivots expand to accommodate that direction in the next month. Traders appreciate that because it supports the cardinal rule of trend trading: "Let your profits run." Similarly, as a market slows, producing smaller ranges, the trader can visualize this easily and adjust his or her trading style.

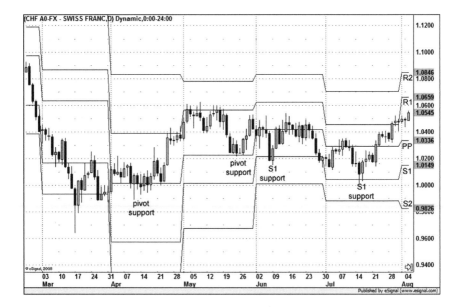

Figure 5-19　Monthly Pivot Points on a Daily USDCHF Chart

Figure 5-19 shows a daily chart of USDCHF in which we can see the influence of the monthly pivots. Notice how in April, after a sharp sell-off in February and March, the market found support on its daily central pivot, which is an indication of underlying strength. A sharp rally followed at the end of April, and after a sell-off in May, support again was found at the daily central pivot. In June and July probes lower were stopped at pivot support 1, as the market put in a second higher low after the overall low of the move it put in during mid-March. Higher lows and a market trading above its central pivot are an indication of strength that could be signaling that the overall bear move in this market is pausing or even reversing.

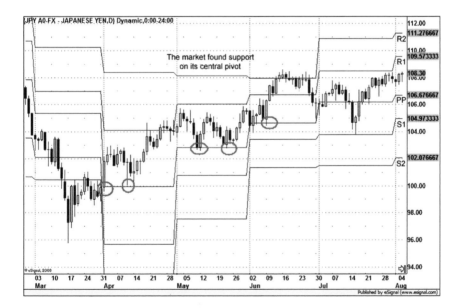

Figure 5-20   Monthly Pivot Points on a Daily USDJPY Chart

Figure 5-20 shows a daily chart of USDJPY in which we see the market put in a succession of higher lows in April, May, and June, which happen to be right on their monthly central pivots. The fact that it tested and found support on pivot support 1 in July and put in another higher low showed the benefit of buying support in an uptrend. June and July provided a good example of the benefits of exiting or selling at R2 and buying at S1 in an uptrend.

Figures 5-21, 5-22, and 5-23 are daily charts in various trending stages, with the monthly pivots overlaid for us to study.

In technical analysis there is no such thing as a good or bad chart to study. There are lessons in all charts covering all time frames. Note how the various markets respond to all the levels,

Figure 5-21   Monthly Pivot Points on a Daily GBPUSD Chart

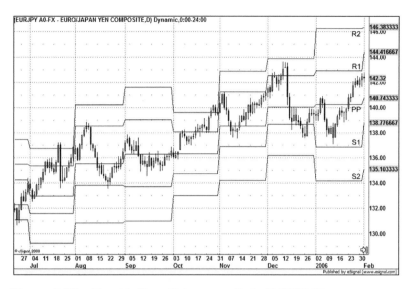

Figure 5-22 Monthly Pivot Points on a Daily EURJPY Chart

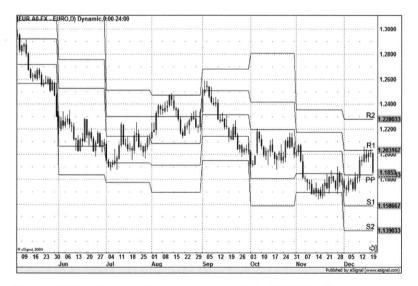

Figure 5-23 Monthly Pivot Points on a Daily EURUSD Chart

not just the central pivots. Also note how whether a market finds support at S1 or resistance at R1 can set the direction going forward. Also, you should start to notice when a market fails to reach a particular level and consider what that is telling you in regard to underlying strength and weakness. We will discuss the concept of buying strength and selling weakness in Chapter 8.

Earlier in the chapter we talked about the validity of the saying "expect corrections." The chart in Figure 5-24 gives us a hint that a correction may be coming. On this 240-minute USDJPY chart we see that the market failed to clear R1 three times and then fell quickly and sliced through its weekly central pivot on July 11, which was a clear warning sign. It struggled to get back above that central pivot the next week,

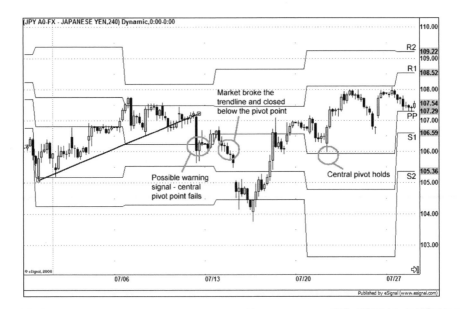

Figure 5-24   Weekly Pivot Points on a 240-Minute USDJPY Chart

giving traders a chance to exit longs or initiate shorts, before falling sharply again. After falling too far too fast without even pausing at S1, the market made a complete recovery ahead of the weekend. The next week it started to sell off again early in the week of July 20, only to retest that weekly central pivot, which held, before moving ahead to post a higher high.

Figure 5-25 shows an example of a buy signal in the form of a bullish engulfing candle, right on the weekly central pivot of this 60-minute USDCHF chart. Not only does the market trading above the weekly pivot tell us that the market is exhibiting underlying strength, the bullish trendline tells us that the market's current direction is higher. The candle clears the high of

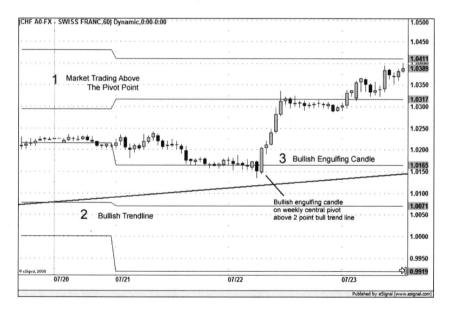

Figure 5-25 Weekly Pivot Points and Bull Trendline on a 60-Minute USDCHF Chart

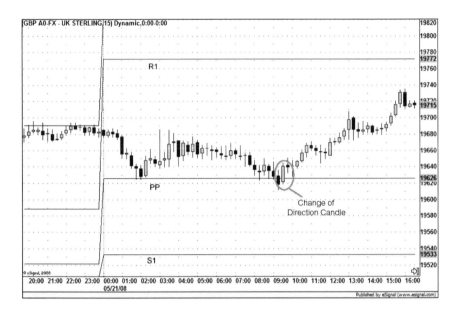

Figure 5-26 Daily Pivot Points on a 15-Minute GBPUSD Chart

the last dozen or more candles, providing a further indication that the buy signal could be a generous one.

Figure 5-26 shows a session in which the market opens above the daily central pivot. We also can see on the far left that on the previous day the British pound challenged R2, which indicates a strong market. For the session on May 21 we see the market trade down to test the central pivot and then give us a bit of a bounce to tell us it respects the pivot, followed by a retest with an actual close below it, before a change-of-direction candle and a close above the central pivot, followed by a nice rally.

In Figure 5-27 we see that the market opens below the weekly central pivot for the week of May 12, 2008. After rallying and

Figure 5-27 Weekly Pivot Points on a 60-Minute Chart in Which Resistance Becomes Support

holding briefly above the pivot, the market fell off hard and traded down to test pivot support 1. After it bottomed just below pivot S1, we see the market start to consolidate above that support level. After trading sideways to slightly higher, it clears a bear trendline angling down from a previous high on May 6, 2008, and we get a nice rally or short-covering correction. The market touches the central pivot one more time just below 196.00 as the week ends. On opening the next week the market is situated above the new central pivot. Remember to "expect corrections." That's what we get here on May 19, and we have to ask ourselves, Is this sell-off a resumption of the previous down move or a correction in a new up move? We don't know. However, we do know that resistance has a tendency to become support, and that's what happens on May 19 as what was previously a resistance trendline becomes a support level. Then we see the market rally up and close above the central pivot on May 20, which is a buy signal. Then we see what happens next as the market wastes little time in rallying up to test pivot R1 on May 20 just below 197.00. Note how a trader would have been rewarded for buying S1 and holding till R2. This tendency happens often in a long-term bull market.

As we've said before, charting and technical analysis are an art, not a science, and sometimes the markets don't play out as cleanly as we'd like them to. There are times when a market will not respect the parameters it lays out for itself, as is demonstrated in Figure 5-28. If the market is not respecting a level, we should not do that either. In Figure 5-28 we see GBPUSD open below the central pivot and then trade above it before falling off and moving along it. The fact that the market cannot give us a bounce off the pivot is showing us that it does not respect that level. At that point, if the market is not respecting that level, we should not respect it either. We also can see that just above the market there is a bear trendline, which is probably why at this time the market is not concerned with possible support at that pivot. We see what price does once it closes below the central pivot, which is sell off steadily. A note on that bear trendline above the market: Trendlines on a chart are a great reminder of a market's current direction, and we should view them the same way we would view a market trading below its central pivot.

A question you may be asking yourself is, "How do I know which pivot point to place importance on: the monthly, weekly,

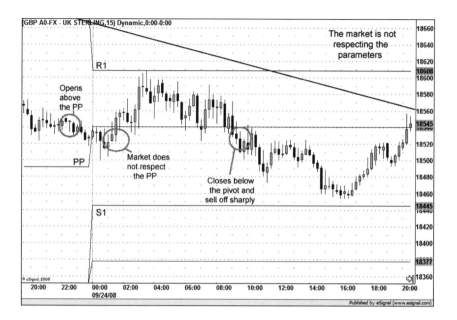

Figure 5-28 Central Pivot Fails to Hold, and Market Slumps

or daily pivot?" The answer is that the time frame you are trading is the pivot point you are going to be watching. If you are position trading by using the daily chart for entry and exits, you are concerned with only the monthly pivots. For trading between a 60-minute and a 240-minute time frame, you follow the weekly pivots, and for day trading, you use the daily pivots. If you are in a trade on a lower time frame and the market outruns the appropriate pivot points, you can consult the next higher time frame's pivots.

Earlier we saw how important previous highs and lows are in creating trendlines and how helpful trendlines are in identifying both long-term and shorter-term trends and support and resistance levels. Now we've also seen how influential pivot points are in providing support and resistance and identifying underlying strength and weakness. We also see how pivots are a trend-following tool in that they expand and contract on the basis of previous market behavior. Next we will look at Fibonacci retracements and extensions to see how they can help us in both trending and countertrending markets.

Fibonacci Retracements and Extensions

In the simplest terms, Fibonacci ratios follow a sequence of numbers and ratios that often are found in nature, such as the uncurling of a fern or the florets of a sunflower. Fibonacci numbers have many applications from mathematics to nature, including advanced analysis of financial market patterns. Many who adhere to behavioral finance point to the measurement of natural psychological patterns that many individuals follow when trading, and Fibonacci ratios provide an explanation of those patterns.

A retracement is a countertrend reaction that retraces a trend. An extension is an impulsive action that continues a trend. Therefore, a Fibonacci retracement is a retracement that fits a Fibonacci ratio and a Fibonacci extension is an extension that fits a Fibonacci ratio. Fibonacci retracements and extensions appear in much more than trading charts and have a strong following among analysts and high-level traders because of their prevalence and repetition in the marketplace. The famed market analyst R. N. Elliot went so far as to call the Fibonacci summation series of numbers and the numerical ratios it creates "the secret of the universe."

The four most common Fibonacci ratios for analysts and traders are 38.2 percent, 50 percent, 61.8 percent, and 100 percent. Here we will focus on Fibonacci retracements and extensions in height, not time. Fibonacci retracements are both a countertrend tool and a trend tool in that they give the trader a potential level for a market retracement to stop at, turn, and resume the overall trend. Fibonacci extensions are a forecasting tool as they take a market move and project into the future a likely area the market will travel to, based on its previous tendencies and on Fibonacci numbers. In today's markets we see 100 percent extensions quite often as well as 0.618 and 1.618 percent extensions. Both retracements and extensions become even more powerful when coupled with a trendline or a significant pivot point. Without a doubt these retracement and extension ratios named after the twelfth-century Italian mathematician are impressive to both analysts and traders. We prefer to wait for a support or resistance level to hold first, then turn, and then give a signal before committing cash to a trade. This means that the level it stops at does not matter as much as does the behavior afterward. Countertrend traders or traders who want a clearly defined risk, however, appreciate the pinpoint accuracy these ratios provide.

A retracement is measured by taking a market move—top to bottom for a down move and bottom to top for an up move—and marking the Fibonacci levels that are deemed significant. Most analysts and traders use 0.382, 0.5, and 0.618, and some include 21 percent and 89 percent.

Figure 5-29 shows a retracement drawn for an up move in USDJPY in April and May 2008. We measure from bottom to top and mark off the 50 percent and 0.618 percent Fibonacci levels. The 50 percent level proves to be significant. As a rule

Figure 5-29 Fifty Percent Retracement Level Holds in USDJPY

of thumb, the smaller the retracement, the stronger the original move. For example, a 0.382 percent retracement after
a move generally indicates a stronger likelihood of a continuation of the original move beyond its previous high or low
compared with a 0.618 retracement. It's also important to note
the distance of the previous retracement, as often that measurement becomes a characteristic and thus repeats itself. As
always, it's very important to have enough information in the
form of time on the chart to avoid being caught measuring
retracements of a minor move or retracements of a retracement
and miss the long-term trend or the big picture.

Figure 5-30 shows how USDJPY falls into a pattern of 0.382
percent retracements as it gives us three in a row. It is not

Figure 5-30 Three 0.382 Percent Retracements in a Row

uncommon to see price movement break down so cleanly into measured retracements. This type of predictability, however, generally is found only in very liquid—that is, very heavily traded—securities, currencies, and commodities.

Figure 5-31 shows GBPUSD completing a perfect 50 percent retracement on a 60-minute chart just ahead of a powerful rally after the U.S. nonfarm payroll news release on June 6, 2008.

Figure 5-32 shows the intersection of a 0.618 percent retracement and a bull trendline hold on a 240-minute chart, followed by a powerful rally that quickly reversed the previous session's sell-off and confirmed the long-term uptrend. Also note the sizable change-of-direction candle that kicked off the up move. In Figure 5-33 we've included a 60-minute chart of the same

Figure 5-31 Fifty Percent Retracement on a 60-Minute GBPUSD Chart after an Economic Release

Figure 5-32 A 0.618 Percent Retracement on a 240-Minute USDJPY Chart

period to highlight the same buy trigger on the next lower time frame.

Figure 5-33 shows the same day we just examined, but on the next lower time frame. Here we again see a change-of-direction candle, this time on the 60-minute chart. Of course we don't know at the time that this intersection of a trendline and a 0.618 percent retracement will hold, but when we see the change-of-direction candle put in the double bottom here, just below 104, we don't think, we buy.

Although Fibonacci retracements are more of a countertrend tool in that they measure primarily corrective price behavior, Fibonacci extensions are a trending tool because they are

Figure 5-33　Intersection of Bull Trendline and 0.618 Percent Retracement in a USDJPY Chart

projecting, or forecasting, targets ahead of the market. An extension would be taken by observing a market move followed by a retracement, measuring the original move, and then taking the same height and extrapolating it up or down from the depth or height of the retracement back in the direction of the longer-term trend by a multiple of 0.618, 1, or 1.618; one also could use any other multiple. To simplify it, we often are looking for a move to repeat itself, or extend 100 percent of itself. This means that if a stock went from 1 to 2 and then back to 1.5, a 100 percent extension of that original move, as measured from the bottom of the retracement or correction at 1.5, would be a move to 2.5.

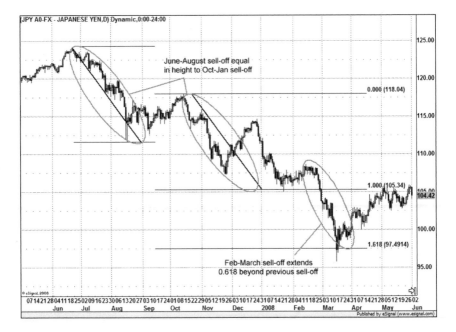

Figure 5-34 Textbook Extensions on a Daily GBPUSD Chart

Figure 5-34 shows a USDJPY chart in which we've measured the June-August sell-off and used the height of that move when taken from the September-October retracement to measure down and give us a target for the next leg lower. We also get a third leg down in February-March, which happens to bottom just below the 1.618 extension given to us from the first leg from the previous summer. Extensions are often effective, just as retracements and other support and resistance levels are, because traders know about them and heed them. For our analysis and trading, we need to know when and where there are significant levels on the chart so that we can take a closer look at price behavior in the short-term time frames at those price levels.

Figure 5-35 A 100 Percent Extension on a Daily USDJPY Chart

Figure 5-35 shows an example of a price move, in this case a rally, followed by a second rally several weeks later of nearly identical height and time. This is a classic case of market symmetry. Note the pattern of higher lows and then the two equal lows in May, which would also be called a double bottom. A double bottom is a classic chart formation that will be covered in the next part of this book. This is a very interesting chart. Note how in early June there was a close above the old May high, or a market "breakout," and USDJPY quickly extended its move to replicate the earlier rally. Studying charts like this during off-market hours in a relaxed environment is great experience for market students.

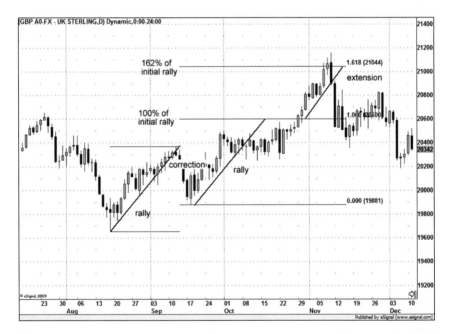

Figure 5-36　A 161.8 Percent Extension on a Daily GBPUSD Chart

Figure 5-36 shows a late summer rally in 2007 in GBPUSD and then a sharp correction lower by approximately 66 percent of the up move into mid-September, which provides a retracement from which to draw an extension higher. In this case the market pulls up short of the 100 percent extension in early October and proceeds to move sideways for much of the month before slipping higher toward the end of the month. The second close above the 100 percent extension proves to be a "breakout" above both that level and the isolated high back in July, and we get a very fast rally, or a climax rally, up to the 1.618 extension level.

Figure 5-37 A 100 Percent Extension on a Daily GBPUSD Chart

The extensions we see most are the 100 percent measurements, and Figure 5-37 shows one on the daily GBPUSD chart after a brief sideways correction in late February-early March 2008.

We have seen how important support and resistance levels are to markets and traders. We see support and resistance in the form of previous daily highs and lows and the trendlines created by them, pivot points on all time frames, and retracement and extension levels. As you can see, there are plenty of levels for traders to be concerned about on a chart, but the most important thing to remember is that we don't respect the level unless the market does that first. Although you may be concerned about having so many lines on your chart, you can relax because as you will see, the markets will tell you which lines are significant. Technical analysis is, after all, an art and is based on the assumption that "the charts tell us everything the market knows about itself." It's up to us to stay loose and keep an open mind so that we can see what the market is telling us.

CHAPTER 6

CHART PATTERNS

Now that we understand how a chart is constructed and how price action identifies significant support and resistance levels, we will discuss chart patterns, which are formations created by multiple support and resistance points and trendlines. Whether we know it or not, pattern-recognition skills play a big part in our lives and those of the people around us. To talk about price patterns on financial charts, we also must cover price volume, which is the total number of actual securities or contracts traded for a particular bar or candle; it tells us whether the trader participation rate is high or low relative to what it has been and whether volume is increasing or decreasing. The candle pattern gives us the length of a price movement, and the volume tells us the size of the participation rate. For securities, commodities, and currency analysis, volume is of particular importance at the potential inflection points in the chart patterns where the trend shifts. Volume is displayed at the bottom of the chart in a histogram and is used to confirm direction. If a breakout, or penetration of an important price level, occurs on rising volume, it is considered more viable; if it occurs on light volume, a continuation in the direction of the breakout is considered less likely.

Although stocks and futures have actual volume indicators available, most platforms for forex markets do not. Some chart packages, however, have tick volume on their intraday forex charts that mimics futures volume and is considered a viable indicator. On some chart packages the volume histogram can be colored; depending on whether the accompanying bar or candle was higher or lower; a green volume histogram would indicate that the candle closed higher than the open and a red volume histogram would indicate that it closed lower.

Like the trendlines and the support and resistance points that create them, chart patterns provide a concise picture of buyer and seller participation. Chart patterns give us an unbiased look at the pricing results of the demand bid for and the supply offered in a market, and volume tells us how much product or money actually changed hands. Technical analysis is an art in which the chart is the canvas, support and resistance lines are the brushstrokes, and patterns or formations are the picture. For our study these patterns can be broken down into two groups: continuation patterns and reversal patterns. Continuation patterns tell us the market probably is pausing, or is in a temporary holding pattern before a resumption of the previous trend. Reversal patterns tell us a trend may be ending and alert us to a potential reversal in direction. Reversal patterns can be broken down into the two subcategories of topping and bottoming patterns. Volume acts as a further confirmation of pattern. For continuation patterns we would expect actual volume to be modest or declining, and for potential reversal patterns we would expect volume to be increasing; this is what we mean when we say that volume confirms direction.

We will be covering the following price patterns:

Continuation Patterns

Bull and bear flag/pennant
Horizontal channel or rectangle
Symmetrical, ascending, and descending triangles
Cup and handle

Reversal Patterns

Double top and double bottom formations
Triple top and triple bottom formations
Head and shoulders top and bottom formations
Rising and falling wedge formations

A quick word on patterns before we cover them individually: A price pattern or formation should jump out at you to be considered valid. It must be obvious to you and other traders for it to be effective. Formations are created from trendlines, and so the same nuances we learned about trendlines—it takes only two points to draw them, and support can become resistance and vice versa—apply to price patterns.

We are going to cover continuation patterns first, because in our trading careers we will see more of these than reversal patterns. It is the nature of markets to trend more than they reverse. We refer to these as continuation patterns, but there is no assurance that they will in fact mark consolidation moves until they actually do so.

Continuation Patterns

Flags

Flags, or pennants as some analysts call them, are short-term continuation patterns that are created when a trending market encounters support (or resistance) in the form of demand (or supply) and price pauses and retraces or goes sideways— i.e., flags—for a short period. A flag often comes in the middle of a move; hence the old trading floor saying "the flag flies at half mast." For a move to be recognized as a flag, there must be a prior trend in place. This prior trend or directional price movement is called the flagpole, and the price objective once the flag is completed is a 100 percent extension of the flagpole from the lowest price on the flag. To visualize what this looks like, the market experiences a trending move, then a brief countertrend move we know to be a flag, and then a second trending move that continues in the same direction as the first. Flag formations are common in many markets, and the stronger the move before the flag is, the more likely it is that we will see the market continue in the original direction and complete the objective.

Figure 6-1 shows an example of a bull flag in the EURUSD in October 2007. We've measured the height or price distance of the flagpole before the flag and then measured a 100 percent extension of that move from the low of the flag. The rally after the bull flag was similar in both length and time.

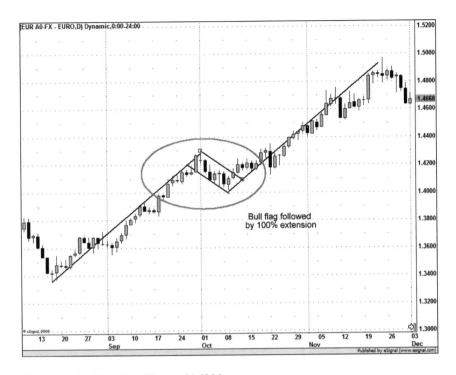

Figure 6-1   The Flag Flies at Half Mast

In the course of an up move or a down move it is common to see a series of flags as the move develops and matures.

Figure 6-2 shows a series of bull flags in USDCHF in which the tick volume is much higher on the rallies than on the flags. This is textbook chart pattern analysis as higher volume is confirming the up moves and lower volume is confirming the countertrend price action, that is, the flags. Note also how the impulse moves, or rallies, are very similar to one another in height and distance. This symmetry is common in chart formations.

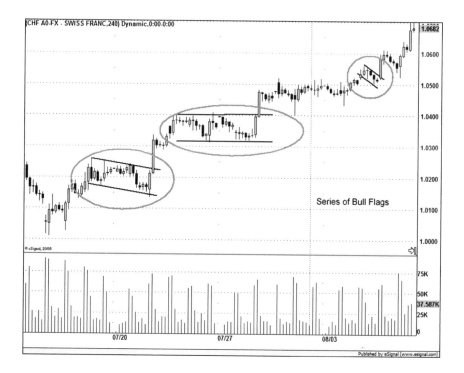

Figure 6-2 Series of Bull Flags on a USDCHD Daily Chart

In Figure 6-3 we see a bear flag in the stock market in 2007 that played out in the Dow Jones futures contracts. The market makes a sharp impulse move down, followed by the flag, and then a second continuation impulse move down. We then get a hammer on the downside target (price objective). As quickly as the July price break came, it was over in August, and for all the economic drama the 1,500-point sell-off brought, we were left with a simple symmetrical

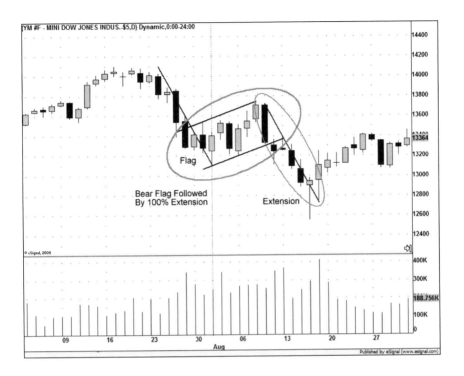

Figure 6-3   Textbook Bear Flag in U.S. Stock Market in August 2007

formation that a student of technical analysis would find predictable.

Figure 6-4 shows a series of orderly bear flags followed by a sharp sell-off on August 7, 2008. Note how the tick volume increased on each individual down bar, followed by volume clusters before the price collapse. In markets we often see an orderly price move to establish direction, then acceleration on increasing volume, followed by a dramatic sell-off.

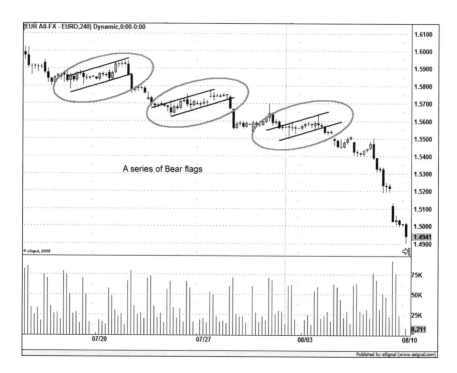

Figure 6-4 Series of Bear Flags on a Daily EURUSD Chart

Horizontal Channel

The rectangle, or horizontal channel, is essentially a sideways trading range that a market creates while consolidating a previous impulse move. It can be thought of as a larger, parallel flag formation. The price objective once the channel is broken is the same as the height of the channel, as can be seen in Figure 6-5. Note how we are seeing the same tendencies in price behavior and price objective over and over in each example. In our experience technical analysis is less complicated than people seem to want to make it.

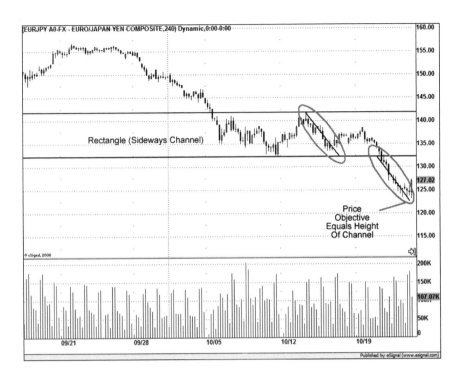

Figure 6-5 Measured Breakdown after a Sideways Channel

Figure 6-6 shows EURJPY pausing and creating a sideways channel before breaking out in the same direction in which it entered the formation. This formation reminds us of the importance of waiting for a close outside the resistance before committing to a trade.

Triangles

A symmetrical triangle is a little more complex than the other continuation patterns. The pattern requires at least two lower

133

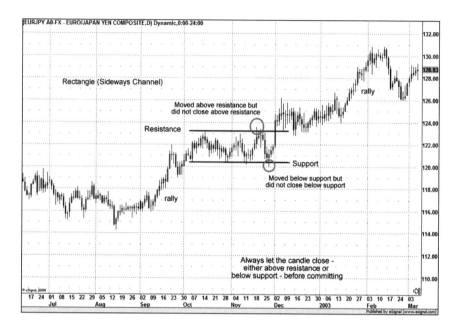

Figure 6-6 Sideways Pause before Resumption of Move

highs and higher lows within the triangle and usually shows three, and it tends to break out of the formation in the same direction in which it was traveling when it created the base. These formations are characteristically larger than flags and take more time to develop. As in any breakout, we must wait for the candle to close outside the formation. There are two different ways to measure the price objective. First, we take the height of the base of the formation; in Figure 6-7 we've marked a thin gray line to mark the base and extrapolated that distance from the breakout or apex of the formation to get the price objective. The other way to determine the objective is to take

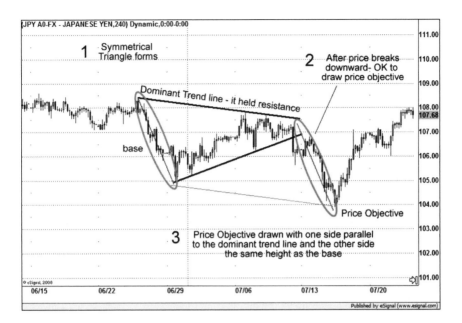

Figure 6-7 Symmetrical Triangle with the Objective Reached

the support or resistance line from which the price broke away—the dominant trendline—and copy or extend it from the base. Both of these measurements give us the same approximate time and price point in July 2008.

We now understand what makes a continuation pattern what it is—price will look to continue in the direction it was moving in before pausing in a pattern—but we also must always remind ourselves that there are times when markets reverse and what starts out looking like a continuation pattern will turn into a reversal pattern. This is why experienced traders always wait for a close above or below the appropriate support or resistance level before committing to a trade.

Two more continuation patterns are the ascending triangle and the descending triangle. The ascending triangle is a bullish formation that more often than not marks a price pause, or consolidation phase, but it can come at the end of a down move and mark a reversal. Wherever they occur on the chart or in the trend, ascending triangles are marked by a horizontal resistance line on top and an angled support line below moving from left to right and connecting higher lows. The rising formation indicates accumulation. Figure 6-8 shows an ascending triangle

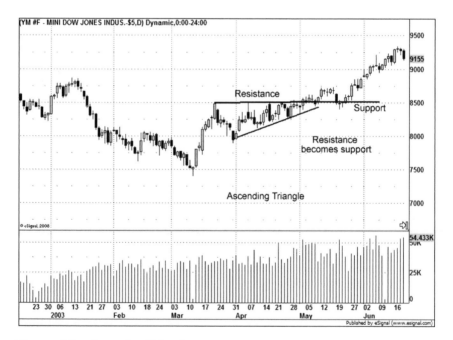

Figure 6-8 Ascending Triangle

in the U.S. stock market in 2003 that stands out nicely on the chart. The hallmark of this formation is its right-angle appearance; it must have at least two high points at the approximate same level and at least two low points, with the most recent being higher than the previous one. As in all technical breakouts, volume should be increasing if there is to be an expected followthrough of the move. The price objective of the formation can be calculated by measuring the base of the triangle and extrapolating that distance from the breakout point.

A descending triangle is a bearish formation that, like an ascending triangle, is more often a continuation pattern, but it

Figure 6-9 Descending Triangle

also can be a reversal pattern. It is a right-angle triangle with at least two low points at approximately the same price level and at least two high points, with the most recent being lower than the previous one. Because of the lower lows of the descending triangle, it has a definite bearish lean even before the breakout. The price objective of the formation can be calculated by measuring the height of the base of the triangle and taking that measurement and extending it down from the breakout point.

Figure 6-9 shows a descending triangle on the USDCHF weekly chart in 2006-2007 that lasted for over a year and a half.

Cup and Handle

The cup and handle (Figure 6-10) is a bullish continuation pattern that is named for its resemblance to a teacup with a handle. The cup is a rounded consolidation pattern that forms after a price advance, and the handle is a bull flag that launches an upside breakout. The depth of the cup generally will not retrace more than half the previous advance, ideally less. There also has to be a marked increase in volume after the price advance from the handle. The minimum price objective of the breakout is equal to the distance from the bottom of the cup to the top of the handle.

Let us remind you again that a chart formation should pop out at you when you glance at the chart. As a rule of thumb, the more obvious the formation is, the more likely it is that it will play out and its price objective will be achieved.

We are going to cover reversal patterns next, and it's important to remember that these topping or bottoming patterns are

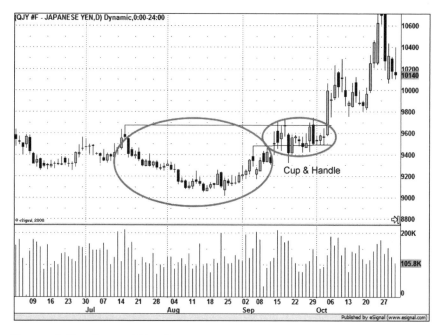

Figure 6-10   Cup and Handle

not nearly as common as continuation patterns. A word of caution is due in addressing reversal patterns, particularly on long-term charts, because they occur less often. There is something in human nature that makes us feel we need to change things for the better. Beginning students imagine that they can discern a change in the market before the rest of us and call a market top or bottom and maximize their profits along the way. Experienced traders know better and are more interested in going along with the market, which means trading through more continuation patterns than reversal patterns. It is best to understand this human tendency to change things at the very beginning of a trading career. The only thing we need to change as traders is our perceptions of our significance in the face of the market.

Reversal Patterns

Double Top and Double Bottom

Double tops and double bottoms are reversal patterns that occur when and where a price meets support or resistance once and then backs off and attempts a second breach before failing and retreating.

A double bottom is a reversal formation marked by two legs at roughly the same price level with a small up move in between on low volume. This bottoming pattern generally occurs at the end of a sustained down move. A double bottom is not confirmed until price closes above the highest price between the two legs (or lows), which is called the breakout point. Volume generally should increase once price closes above the breakout point for the price to move higher and achieve its objective. The price objective for the formation is an up move equal to the height from the lowest leg to the highest point between the legs. A double bottom creates a strong support level.

Figure 6-11 shows the symmetry created by a double bottom in USDCAD in 2001 as price reached its objective and conformed around that level.

A double top is a powerful reversal pattern that can occur at the end of a sustained up move and signal an intermediate-term or even long-term change in the previous trend. The formation is identified by twin peaks with a price dip between them.

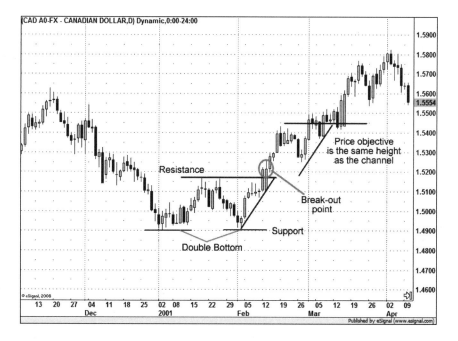

Figure 6-11 Double Bottom

The double top is confirmed when price closes below the lowest point between the peaks, which is called the breakout point. The downside price objective of this formation is the same as the distance between the highest high and the low between the peaks when extrapolated down from that breakout point. As with all reversal patterns, we need to see volume increasing from the point of the breakout to gauge the legitimacy of the coming move. The higher the volume is, the more likely it is that the breakout will continue. Figure 6-12 shows a classic double top in the U.S stock market in May 2008.

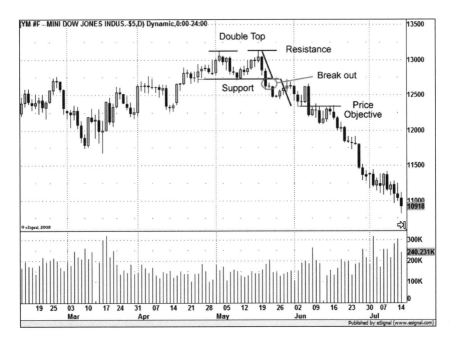

Figure 6-12   Double Top

Triple Top and Triple Bottom

Triple tops and triple bottoms are longer-term reversal patterns that often play out on charts with higher time frames and can mark major trend changes. They can resemble other patterns such as double bottoms or tops or descending or ascending triangles, but as with all formations, a trader should consider them neutral until a breakout comes.

Triple bottoms are created after an extended down move when there are three roughly equal low legs in a market before a rally is mounted from the third leg that shows enough strength to break above the tops of the previous up moves and reverse the course of the market from down to up. The price objective for this reversal pattern is the same as the height from the lowest low to the highest point between the lows before the breakout; it is identical to the measured price objective of a double bottom. Similarly, the breakout has to occur on higher than usual volume for a trader to expect follow-through. As in most technical formations, there is always the likelihood that after the breakout price will pull back one more time to retest the area and resistance will turn into support. Figure 6-13 shows a triple bottom in EURUSD in 2002 in which after the breakout the market came back to retest the last high between

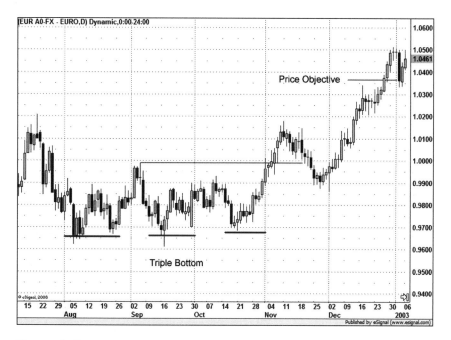

Figure 6-13 Triple Bottom

the second and third lows a month later before turning higher for good to kick off a major rally.

Triple tops are created after an extended up move when there are three roughly equal high points or peaks in a market before a major sell-off is mounted from the third peak that shows enough strength to break below the lows of the down moves between the peaks and reverses the course of the market from up to down, or from bull to bear. The price objective for this reversal pattern is the same as the height from the highest high to the lowest point between the peaks before the breakout; this is identical to the measured price objective of a double top. Similarly,

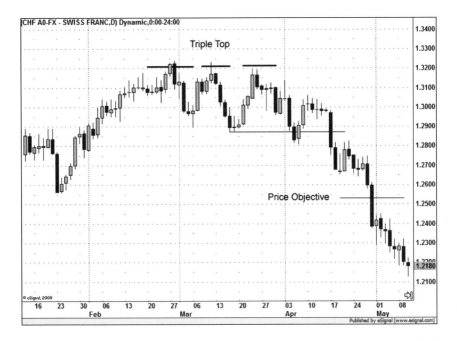

Figure 6-14   Triple Top

the breakout has to occur on higher than usual volume for a trader to expect follow-through.

In Figure 6-14 we see a triple top play out in USDCHF in 2006 and are reminded that what looks obvious can be tricky to trade. There is an initial downside breakout in early April, but then price climbs back above the previous support and rallies slightly before holding for five days in mid-April, giving us two inside candles, before breaking out below for a second time. This reminds us that charting is an art. Once we get the second breakout, the market, true to the characteristic it just showed, comes back one more time to retest the breakout in late April before falling off for good.

Head and Shoulders Tops and Bottoms

Similar to triple bottoms and tops, head and shoulders bottoms and tops are long-term reversal patterns or formations that come at the end of extended market moves and indicate a change in direction for the primary trend for that period.

A head and shoulders bottom, or inverted head and shoulders, marks the bottom of an extended down move and is identified by a distinct pattern similar to the head and shoulders of an upside-down individual. The pattern is created by a sell-off to a new low in a bear market, followed by a modest rally or correction that flags out against the downtrend and fades into another sell-off that leads to another lower low that eventually evolves into the head. Once a potential head is in place, volume starts to pick up as experienced traders begin to buy the market to close out existing short positions. We now have the left shoulder and the head in place while the chart still is showing an existing down move in place, although with lower volume on the last leg down. We now get a rally off the new low on higher volume than we would be seeing for a flag, or bear market, reaction, and this starts to tip us off that a bottoming formation may be building. Once this small rally runs its course, there is one more run down on light volume, which stalls out before testing the lowest low in place. This last run down puts in the right shoulder, and if it is to become a bona fide head and shoulders bottom, it will be obvious on the chart. The breakout level for this formation is called the neckline and can be drawn by connecting the highs put in before the creation of the left shoulder and connecting that trendline to the high created after the creation of the head. Increasing volume, or a higher trader participation rate, plays a key role in the actual breakout stage from the neckline of the formation, as it does in all reversing patterns.

In Figure 6-15 we see a head and shoulders formation in the Dow Jones Industrial Average futures market on a 60-minute chart in August 2008 that tips us off that the current down move in this time frame has run its course. There are two ways to measure the price objective of this formation. The first is to take the distance from the bottom of the head to the neckline and extrapolate the same distance up from the breakout point on the neckline. The second is to take the same distance from the low point of the head to the neckline and extrapolate that up from the highest point on the neckline. In the case of a horizontal neckline these two would be the same; however, when there is an angled neckline, we would have two objectives, with one being higher than the other.

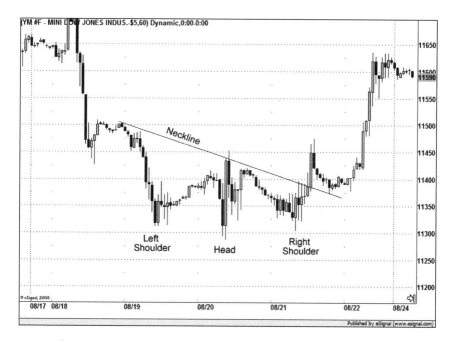

Figure 6-15 Head and Shoulders Bottom

Head and shoulders tops mark the top of an extended up move and are identified by a distinct pattern similar to the head and shoulders of an upright individual. The same points used in describing the head and shoulders bottom apply to the top. The neckline break is the most critical test, as it is this breach that confirms the pattern, or formation. It is important to understand the order of operation of the formation as it evolves from an uptrend, or bull market, to a downtrend, or bear market. The market will go through subtle changes as we see volume go from increasing on the rallies and decreasing on the reactions to decreasing on the rallies and increasing on the sell-offs or price breaks. It is this dynamic occurrence, or behavioral change, that experienced traders can see. This often is referred to as "feeling" a market, as in "that last leg up didn't feel right to me." Even without seeing the volume histogram at the bottom of the chart, experienced traders notice when a market is starting to waver at minor resistance levels or drops faster than it had been dropping on reactions. Head and shoulders formations are great times to notice these subtle changes in price behavior because, like triple tops and triple bottoms, they take time to play out, giving us time to observe and understand the changing dynamics.

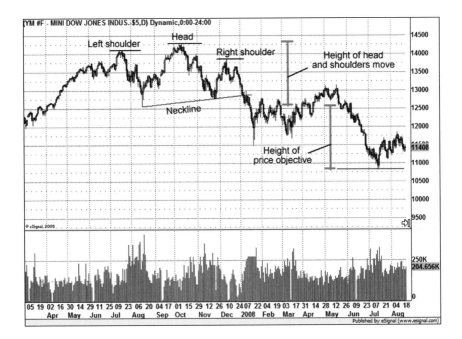

Figure 6-16   Head and Shoulders Top

Figure 6-16 shows a head and shoulders top in the U.S. stock market that played out in 2007 and 2008. We can see from the volume pattern on the chart how trader participation dried up for the last leg up to create the head and then picked up as the market sold off in November. By the time price penetrated the neckline, there was little doubt about who was in control of this market from the price action and volume: the bears. After a climactic sell-off in January, the market snapped back and retested the original breakout area.

Rising and Falling Wedges

A rising wedge is a bearish formation that usually is seen as a reversal pattern but also can be a continuation pattern. Here we will focus on reversal patterns. A rising wedge can be seen on the charts as an up move with a wide shape that gradually narrows as it rises, giving it a cone shape. It can be tricky to identify as being bearish because it exhibits the higher lows and higher highs that are the hallmark of an uptrend. What helps us identify it as a reversal formation is the decreasing volume on each successive rally. Regardless of whether we see it as a bearish development, by following basic trendline analysis we will be able to see when the formation breaks out, or down, by the way it penetrates the support line that helps identify it. Figure 6-17 shows a rising wedge on the weekly USDCAD chart that built up through the second half of 2001 and culminated with a major reversal in early 2002.

A falling wedge is a bullish formation that usually is seen as a reversal pattern but also can be a continuation pattern. Here we will focus on reversal patterns. It can be seen on the

Figure 6-17 Rising Wedge

charts as a down move with a wide shape that gradually narrows as it falls, giving it a cone shape. Like a rising wedge, it can be tricky to identify as being bullish because of the lower highs and lower lows. Again, what helps us identify it as a reversal formation is the decreasing volume on each successive sell-off. By following trendline analysis, we should be able to identify the breakout or point of reversal when it penetrates the resistance line that borders its upper range. There is no way to project a price objective for this formation. Figure 6-18 shows a falling wedge on a weekly EURJPY chart

Figure 6-18 Falling Wedge

that culminates with a double bottom in the fourth quarter of 2000 just before a powerful reversal and rally.

The pattern-recognition techniques we've outlined can come in handy in analyzing and trading the financial markets. When taken in the context of the candlestick charts, support and resistance levels, and trendlines we have studied, the prospect of forecasting market movement should start to seem like a very real possibility. Knowing that we are likely to see price continuation patterns more often than actual price reversal patterns should give us an edge over less educated analysts and traders. In summary, we can say that basic price patterns and volume indicators are essential in the study of technical analysis and will bring us closer to melding market analysis with our intuition.

CHAPTER 7

TECHNICAL
INDICATORS

A myriad of technical tools, studies, and overlays are available to analysts and traders, and it is our goal to define those which are readily available on most charting packages and those which we use or know are used by other professionals in the trading community. In this section we will cover only those indicators which are derived from price. A technical indicator is a tool that uses a series of data points and various mathematical formulas to define a perspective on market behavior. The primary data points used are an individual period's open, high, low, and closing price. Despite what most analysts believe, technical indicators were not designed to predict future price movement as much as to define current price movement. Each type of indicator has a different formula and varies in its degree of sophistication. It is believed by most experienced money managers and traders that the simplest formulas often lead to the most successful trading.

Leading and Lagging Indicators

The term *leading indicator* is somewhat of a misnomer in that there is no tool that can predict what will happen in the future. Previous and current price behaviors are generally the only determinants in technical analysis. For the sake of analysis, however, technical indicators can be divided into two types: leading indicators and lagging indicators. A leading indicator gives us an indication or signal before an actual price reversal; a lagging indicator gives us an indication or signal after a new trend has started. The first thing one needs to understand about this concept is that trades that are based on a leading indicator probably are going to have a higher losing percentage because the indicator is anticipating price behavior. In contrast, with a lagging indicator we wait for behavior that indicates that a reversal has occurred, and that new trend is already under way before we commit to a trade. Most leading indicators measure momentum, or the degree of the slope of a current price movement—i.e., the speed of the trend—and are called momentum oscillators. Momentum in markets ebbs and flows, and an indicator that lets us know whether the speed of the market is accelerating or slowing is a handy tool to have because larger price changes usually are accompanied by higher price momentum. A market can be making lower lows and lower highs and be in an obvious downtrend, but if the rate of its descent is slowing and we have a position that is going with the trend, we may want to pay closer attention to price. We would take additional confirmation from individual candle behavior and support lines. Similarly, if the rate of acceleration is increasing in our favor, we would be more inclined to maintain our position.

Direction constitutes important information, but measuring momentum, particularly as a market approaches support or resistance, has predictive value. Leading indicators include stochastics, the Relative Strength Index (RSI), and the Commodity Channel Index (CCI). Most trend-following indicators, or "overlays," such as moving averages and moving average crosses, are considered lagging indicators as they are giving us the price's previous and current direction. Indicators based on previous price action cannot alert us to a change of direction until after the market has experienced it. An advantage of this is that we are inclined to stay with positions longer. It is thought by many experienced traders that the most important skill a trader can have and the one that is the hardest to achieve is the ability to "let a profit run," or stay in a position longer and maximize profits. Two of the main reasons for this are emotions, generally nervousness, and leading indicators. Trend traders need to be comfortable with lagging indicators. Lagging indicators other then moving averages include moving average convergence/divergence (MACD) and Bollinger bands.

Lagging Indicators

Moving Averages and Crosses: Simple and Exponential

Moving averages are lagging indicators that are overlaid on the price chart and are used primarily to help traders identify a trend's direction, provide support or resistance, and generate trade signals. A simple moving average (SMA) is a chart overlay that provides a smoothed average of the closing prices or opening prices for a particular period. A simple moving average is calculated by adding together a specific number of bars' or candles' closing prices and dividing that sum by the total number of time periods to get an average price. The formula for a five-period moving average is

$$SMA = (C1 + C2 + C3 + C4 + C5) \div 5$$

Figure 7-1 shows a five-period simple moving average taken for EURUSD in summer 2008. As each candle is completed on the chart, a new average point is plotted so that over time the average moves forward, following price. The shorter-term the time frame covered by the moving average is, the more sensitive the moving average becomes and the choppier the line becomes. The longer-term the moving average is, the more

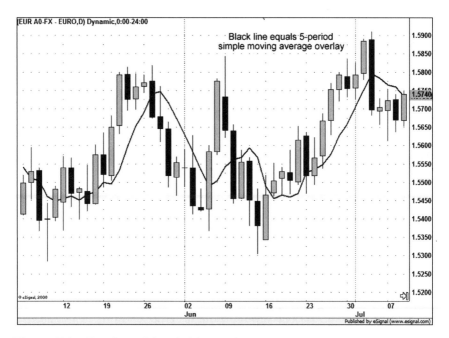

Figure 7-1   Five-Period Simple Moving Average

desensitized it becomes and the smoother the line becomes. The moving average is used to smooth out actual price action in an effort to make the trend easier to spot. When price is trading above the moving average points, the trend is said to be higher, whereas price trading below the moving average indicates that the trend is lower. Some analysts use longer-term moving averages such as 100-period and 200-period averages as support or resistance. Longer-term averages also are used to generate signals in several ways. If the close is above or below a particular moving average, a buy or sell signal may be generated. A moving average cross is formed by using two separate averages that are based on two different time frames that then are used both to confirm trending price action and to generate trade signals. Figure 7-2 is a chart of the S&P 500 stock index futures contract from the fourth quarter of 2007 through

Figure 7-2   Fifty-Period and 200-Period Simple Moving Average

the third quarter of 2008 with a 50-period and a 200-period simple moving average overlay.

When the shorter-term average crosses below the longer-term one, it is a sell signal and the trend is presumed to be down; similarly, when the shorter-term average crosses above the longer-term one, it is a buy signal and the trend is said to be up. Similarly, if price is above the moving averages, the trend is said to be up, and if price is below the moving averages, it is down.

The cross of the 50-day SMA below the 200-day SMA in late December 2007 in Figure 7-2 provides a well-timed sell trigger. Such long-term averages are not sensitive and will keep you in a trade for an extended period; that can be trying, as was the case in March through May when the market rallied but rewarding from mid-May till mid-July as the market fell off and made a new low for the year. Note how the 50-day SMA provided a pivotal level in March and April and again in late May and how the 200-day SMA provided a good resistance level in May. Professionals tend to use 50-day and 200-day SMAs when they are analyzing or trading securities.

The exponential moving average (EMA) is a moving average overlay that puts more weight on the most recent closing prices to make it more responsive to newer incoming price data. Currency traders often use 89-period and 144-period exponential moving averages simultaneously for their long-term charts, considering a crossover of the two averages an important signal. When the shorter-term average crosses below the longer-term one, it is a sell signal and the trend is presumed to be down; when the shorter-term average crosses above the longer-term one, it is a buy signal and the trend is said to be up. Similarly, when price is above the moving averages, the trend is considered up, and when price is below the moving averages, the trend is considered down.

It is important to remember that moving averages and their crosses are lagging indicators, meaning that the trend must change before the longer-term moving average crosses will confirm it. Thus, they are more suited for trading longer-term, and traders who use them should be prepared to weather significant drawdowns as they often give a signal after a large move, leaving the position open in the face of initial corrections. It is important to understand that it is at the beginning of trend changes that corrections and price swings tend to be at their biggest, making the longer-term averages and crosses more analytic tools than trading tools for more experienced traders. Long-term exponential moving averages also are used as support or resistance levels.

Figure 7-3   An 89-Period and a 144-Period Exponential Moving Average Cross

In Figure 7-3 we have an 89-period and a 144-period EMA cross that generates a sell signal on the daily chart. This signal proved very profitable 18 months later, but it gave the trader a sizable drawdown 6 months into the trade. Another way moving averages can prove useful is by acting as support or resistance levels once a trend is established, as can be seen in Figure 7-3 when the moving averages provide resistance in August and September 2007.

A drawback of moving averages is that they can distract a trader from focusing on simple isolated highs and lows and trendlines, which give a trader excellent information in a timely manner.

Oscillators

An oscillator is a set of data that moves back and forth, or oscillates, between two points. The oscillators we will discuss in this chapter are MACD, stochastics, RSI, CCI, and parabolic stop and reverse (SAR).

MACD

The moving average convergence/divergence (MACD) is a versatile indicator that combines a trend-following function with a centered oscillator, also known as a momentum indicator. By developing MACD, a derivative of moving averages, Gerald Appel gave us a hybrid tool that is helpful in determining present direction and measures momentum (the rate of change in price). Although it may look very similar to a moving average, the MACD is actually a tool that shows the divergence of two moving averages. The parameters of the MACD are expressed as follows:

MACD "A, B, C"

where

A = the number of bars in the fast moving average
B = the number of bars in the slow moving average
C = the number of bars used to calculate the difference between the two averages

A typical MACD ratio is 12, 26, 9. The change of two moving averages either closer to or farther away from each other has predictive value. As the moving averages approach each other in value, a potential crossover may be forming, meaning that the momentum of the current trend is slowing and the market may be getting ready to change trend direction. Similarly, as a trend strengthens, the moving averages grow farther apart, indicating an increase in momentum. In Figure 7-4, the MACD is shown at the bottom of a price chart. Note that there is both a linear component and a histogram component (shown as a series of vertical bars). The black line represents the MACD, which is the average of the differences between two moving averages. The heavy line is the fastest-moving component. The lighter line is an average of the MACD over nine periods, and it is a slower-moving component. The two lines move closer to and farther away from each other over time, and occasionally they cross. The histogram shows the variation in the distance between the fast-moving and slow-moving components and makes

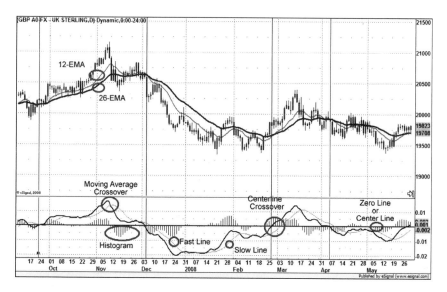

Figure 7-4 Construction of the MACD

crossovers easier to visualize. When the MACD was introduced, it consisted of only the MACD line. The trigger line and the histogram components were added later by Thomas Aspray.

The MACD histogram measures momentum. When the bars on the histogram are moving away from zero, that is interpreted as positive momentum; when they are moving toward the zero line, momentum is decreasing. Positive momentum indicates that the current trend is strengthening, and negative momentum indicates that it is weakening. A shift in the MACD histogram, such as a decrease after a series of increases in a price uptrend or an increase after a series of decreases in a price downtrend, can be seen as the first indication of a potential shift in price direction, or trend.

The MACD and MACD histogram generate buy or sell signals, or trade filters, in several different ways, including

MACD centerline crossover, MACD moving average crossover, MACD histogram shift, and both MACD and MACD histogram divergence.

MACD Centerline Crossover

A centerline crossover occurs when the black MACD line crosses over the zero line, or centerline. For the GBPUSD chart in Figure 7-4, which covers the last quarter of 2007 and the first five months of 2008, we have overlaid the 12-period and 26-period moving averages so that you can visualize one aspect of what the MACD is showing: a crossover of the 12-period and 26-period moving averages. The black line of the MACD moving below the zero line coincides with the 12-period average moving below the 26-period average, both of which are sell signals. The black line of the MACD moving above the zero line generates a buy signal. It is this zero line cross that represents an important indication, as we can see from the direction GBPUSD took after these signals in 2007 and 2008.

MACD Trigger Line Crossover

Figures 7-5 and 7-6 show the MACD as it crosses over its trigger line; this is known as a moving average crossover or an MACD cross. When the MACD is below its trigger line, it supports a short position; when it is above the trigger line, it supports a long position. The MACD crossing its trigger line can be useful for identifying price extremes and can be used to exit trend trades and enter countertrend trades. Combined with the oscillator function, a crossover of the two lines in proximity to the zero line

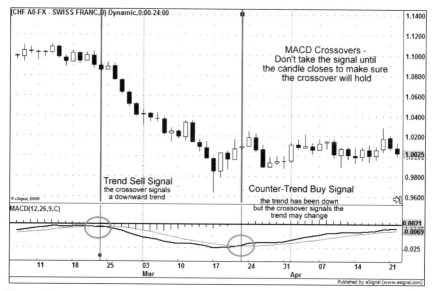

Figure 7-5 MACD Trigger Line Cross

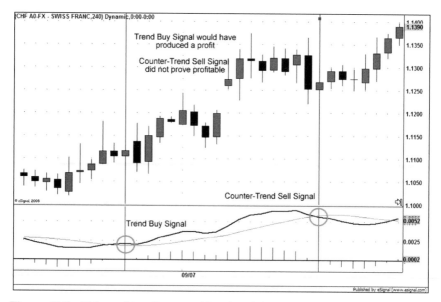

Figure 7-6 Trigger Line Cross as Trend and CounterTrend

provides additional information about whether a trigger is i direction of the current trend. A black line cross below the gray line that occurs below the zero line would indicate a sell signal in the direction of the predominant trend, whereas a black line cross above the gray line below the zero line would be a countertrend buy signal. Figure 7-5 is a daily chart of USDCHF from late winter to early spring 2008.

When there is a black line cross above the gray line above zero, it is a trend buy signal; a black line cross below the gray line above zero is a countertrend sell signal. Figure 7-6 shows a 240-minute chart of USDCHF from September 2007. Thus, although the zero line cross by the black line is still the most influential signal because it is a trending signal, we also have the MACD-trigger line cross, which can be both a trend signal and a countertrend signal.

MACD Histogram

The rate of change between the two lines (the MACD and the trigger line) also provides an indication of the strength of a move and is represented by the vertical bars, or histograms, that populate the centerline of the indicator. If the distance between the two lines is increasing, the move under way is considered strong and the histogram will be marked by successively higher bars; if the distance between the two lines is decreasing, the momentum of the move is waning and the histogram will record shorter bars. This information is valuable in deciding to let a profit run if the MACD histogram is increasing in the direction of a trade. Similarly, if you are in a trade and the histogram is moving against your position, it is a warning that price momentum is starting to work against your position.

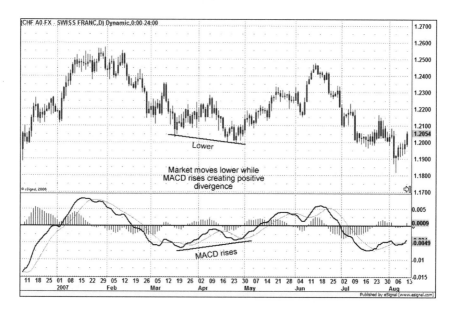

Figure 7-7 Positive Divergence as Measured by MACD

MACD Divergence

Another way the MACD functions is to show signals called divergence. Divergence occurs when a price is going in one direction and the MACD or another momentum-measuring indicator is not confirming that direction. Price can be making lower lows, but if the rate of change is slowing over time, it will show up as higher lows or even a flattening MACD. This can telegraph a price pause or even a price reversal. This is known as positive divergence between price and the MACD. Figure 7-7 shows an example of positive divergence in the USDCHF in spring 2007.

Negative divergence occurs when price is still rising but the MACD and the trigger line are moving sideways or falling.

In strong market moves it is not uncommon to see double or even triple divergence before seeing a significant correction or reversal. As a rule of thumb, divergence over a shorter period is more powerful than divergence over a longer period. Think of divergence as a development that indicates that a market needs to take a break. It is reasonable to consider that there will be times in a bear market when a market becomes oversold, momentum starts to wane, and a correction is needed. Price technically still is moving lower, but momentum is slowing. Price may backtrack and test resistance before continuing on. Although most market reversals exhibit divergence before they turn, they also exhibit this behavior just before normal consolidation periods.

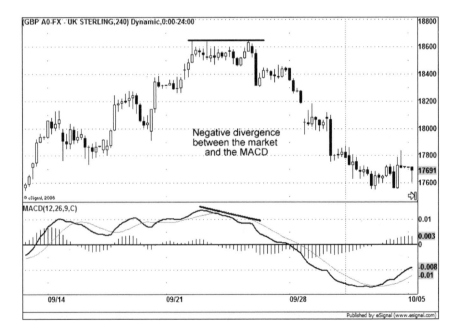

Figure 7-8 Negative Divergence as Measured by MACD

In Figure 7-8, which is a 240-minute chart of GBPUSD from September 2008, we have an example of negative divergence before a market turn and sell-off.

Figure 7-9, a chart of EURJPY from the second half of 2006, shows the many roles MACD can play in market analysis. We see a prominent resistance level just above 150.00. The market is respecting both the bull trendline and the resistance level. In September and October the market goes flat and starts to wrap around its monthly central pivot in black. In early November it's safe to say that we don't know which way the market will break out. The MACD, however, did give us a hint of the rally to come by staying above the zero level. Note also how once the rally kicked off in earnest in late November, the

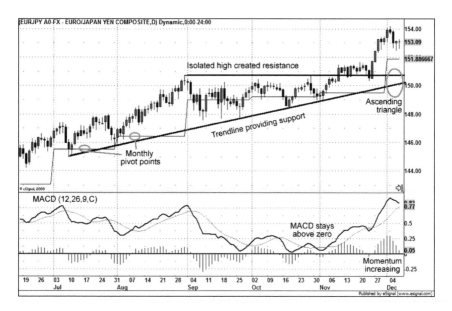

Figure 7-9 MACD and Support and Resistance

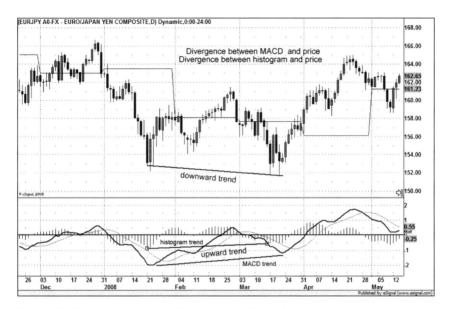

Figure 7-10 Divergence on MACD and MACD Histogram

MACD accelerated away from the trigger line. This shows that the difference between the two lines was increasing. This was a powerful signal telling traders to maintain their long positions. After reading about chart patterns, we can see that in Figure 7-9 there is an ascending triangle, which is a bullish continuation pattern.

In our analysis we also will see divergence between the MACD histogram and price. Just as the divergence between price and the MACD line can be significant, the divergence between the histogram and price also can be significant (see Figure 7-10).

Traders often ask, "Which divergence should we look for, that between the MACD cross (the black and gray lines) and price or that between the MACD histogram and price?" The answer is either one; however, short-term divergence generally will show up first on the histogram and can be more significant.

After gauging the current price trend on the chart, we look for the direction of the MACD to confirm that trend. We gauge the momentum of that trend through the MACD histogram. We are also aware of which side of the zero line MACD is on. For trade signals we want to have the MACD histogram moving in the same direction as the trade. Once in the trade, we monitor the MACD histogram, and if momentum exists, we stay in the trade to let the profit run. If we get a MACD cross against our position on the same time frame we took the signal on, we almost certainly will take that as a signal to exit the trade.

To summarize, we use the MACD to identify trends as well as possible turning points or shifts in momentum and to keep us in a trend trade longer. For countertrend trades we look for divergence between the MACD and/or the MACD histogram and price. Before entering a trade, we always want to know the MACD's stance relative to the zero line and the direction of the MACD and its trigger line.

Bollinger Bands

Bollinger bands were developed by John Bollinger as a way to incorporate volatility and price by using an 18-period simple moving average to help define price and trend and a 2 standard deviation measurement both added to and subtracted from the 18-period SMA to gauge potential volatility. This tool is made up of three bands that are used in an attempt to encompass the majority of a market's price action. The number of periods in an SMA and the width of the standard deviations are variables that can be changed in accordance with your trading plan to give wider or tighter ranges. Because a simple moving average is at the center of this market overlay, this is considered a lagging indicator.

Bollinger bands generally are not known as a signal-generating tool but as a trading aid for identifying low volatility or ranging periods in a market and for identifying price extremes brought on by high volatility. A narrowing of the bands can identify a market that may be one to watch for a breakout. Widening of the bands or high volatility is seen when price penetrates the outer band, and that can be interpreted as a hint to take a profit or exit a market that may be approaching unsustainable levels for that particular period. When price closes above or below the moving average at the center of the bands—generally an 18-SMA or 20-SMA—this can be taken as a directional bias.

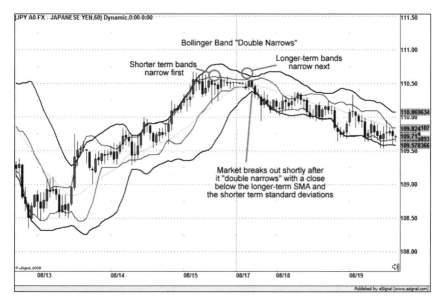

Figure 7-11 Bollinger Bands with Double Narrows

You also can layer two different Bollinger bands on the same price chart by adjusting the SMA and the standard deviation measurement. By coupling a shorter time frame EMA that has smaller deviations with an 18-SMA that has a 2 standard deviation Bollinger band, we may be tipped off sooner that a desirable setup is in the making. Figure 7-11 shows a shorter-term Bollinger band in gray narrow down ahead of the longer-term Bollinger band in black. The double narrows is telling us that the flow, or volatility, is likely to pick up in the coming candles, or bars, which it does.

Bollinger bands are useful in that an analyst or trader can scan any number of charts and markets in a short time in an effort to home in on setups she finds favorable on the basis of her experience.

Parabolic Stop and Reverse

The parabolic stop and reverse (parabolic SAR) is a tool for setting a trailing stop; it was created by Welles Wilder, the developer of the RSI. The calculation used is too complex to cover here, but the concept is very simple. The SAR indicator provides a dotted line above or below price to place your stop to either exit a position or enter a new position, that is, stop and reverse. There are two variables for setting up the indicator. The first is the step, which calculates where the stop initially should be placed, and the second is the maximum step, which controls the increment adjustment of the SAR point as price moves. Wilder suggested a step setting of 0.02 and a maximum step setting of 0.20, and that is what most charting packages default to. The higher the step setting is, the more sensitive the price point will be.

Wilder recommended identifying the trend in a market before employing this indicator. In a primary uptrend a buy stop signal is given when price trades up through the indicated SAR point, and in a downtrend a sell stop signal is given when price trades down through the SAR price point.

Once you initiate a position, the new stop level should be fairly loose, giving the market room to breathe while maintaining a safe distance from the position. As the move gets under way, however, the SAR will tighten up the stop price point.

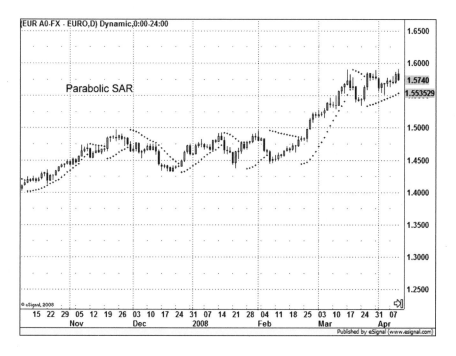

Figure 7-12   Parabolic SAR

Figure 7-12 demonstrates how the parabolic SAR is a simple, straightforward way to determine a valid level to place a stop with one mouse stroke.

Leading Indicators

Stochastic Oscillator

A stochastic oscillator is another form of oscillator that measures momentum and is based on the relationship of the closing price to the price range. Stochastic oscillators provide an excellent view of trending and the strength of a trend. The mechanics behind the stochastics show that when there is a strong uptrend, the prices are closing near the top of the price range and the stochastic value is above 75. In a strong downtrend, the prices are closing near the bottom of the range and the stochastic value is below 25. The parameters of 75 and 25 are variable, and most traders use values between 70 and 80 and between 20 and 30.

We use a slow stochastic, which like all centered oscillators is a momentum indicator and is considered a leading indicator. It takes its determinants from the most recent closing price relative to the high range and low range over a specific period. There are two components to the oscillator: a line referred to as %K (the "fast" line) and another called %D (the "slow" dashed line). The math behind these calculations is rather complex, and all charting packages have the stochastic already calculated; thus, we won't waste time analyzing how the values are derived.

We recommend using a 14-day %K, which is based on the most recent close and the price range over the last 14 candles.

We use a three-day simple moving average of %K to arrive at %D. The %D functions as a "trigger" line. Notice the similarity to the MACD model, in which the trigger line is a derivative of the MACD average. As a result of the fact that the trigger line is based on a shorter time period (three days), the stochastic is a very sensitive indicator. We also place an oversold line between 20 and 30 and an overbought line between 70 and 80 on the chart. George Lane, who developed this indicator, believed that some of the best signals come after the indicator has risen above the upper level and then comes back down through that level or after it has fallen through the lower level and rises back up through that level. Like all momentum indicators, it shows divergence with price, which aids in trade selection. We use the slow stochastic to alert us to a possible trade setup and use a cross above or below the oversold or overbought line as a trade signal. We also can use a stochastic crossover of the trigger line as an alert that a trade signal may be following, particularly if it happens on a chart with a higher time frame. We also use the stochastic as a tool to help identify a market's short-term trend, which we will cover in Chapter 9 in the section on quantifying trends.

Figure 7-13 provides a good example of a stochastic confirming a change-of-direction candle sell signal right on the previous session's high, which is marked in gray. The sell given by the stochastic in the form of a cross and close below 75 is a countertrend signal, which we would determine because it was counter to the direction of the black trendline below the price action. What happened here was that price had rallied away from the bull trendline, and with no more buying to propel it higher, professional traders took the opportunity to book a profit on their trend trades (and closed out their positions). The stochastic gave the sell

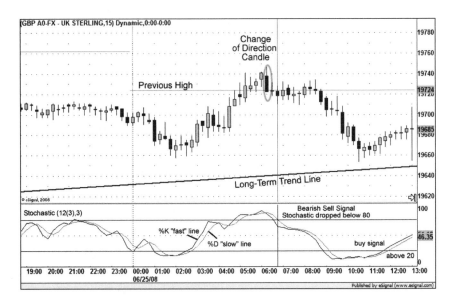

Figure 7-13   Stochastic Sell Signal Precludes Pullback and Test of Bull Trendline

indication on the candle that closed below the low of the change-of-direction candle; that proved to be very good timing, as price leveled off and then slumped back down to that longer-term bull trendline. The stochastic is a sensitive indicator and is almost always one of the first technical indicators to turn. If this indicator had remained above the overbought line, it would have told us that the short-term trend remained higher.

Stochastics, like other technical indicators, are only tools, and we would never trade specifically off these signals; instead, we use them in conjunction with trendline violations, candle formations, and of course support or resistance levels. Because a stochastic is so sensitive, it is a good indicator to use for signal generation that gets you in quickly. A very good short-term signal that we will cover in Chapter 12 in the material on trade

Figure 7-14   Stochastic Identifies Negative Divergence

signals occurs when we see a combination of a trendline violation and a stochastic cross. We also can use the stochastic to
identify divergence, as is illustrated in Figure 7-14.

Some traders also use a stochastic in their short-term trading by taking a close above 70 as a buy signal and a close below
30 as a sell signal. This may seem counterintuitive initially but
can work well in identifying markets that are accelerating.
Another way to use the signal is to wait for a second cross
down from the upper level or a second cross up through the
lower level before entering a position. The stochastic is a sensitive indicator, and by seeking out markets in which it gives
that second cross for a signal, it is thought that a trader can
help increase the odds of success on a trade.

177

The stochastic is a timely indicator that helps identify trend and countertrend signals, as well as price extremes, shifts in momentum, and divergence in trends.

Relative Strength Index

The Relative Strength Index is a momentum oscillator/leading indicator that is based on the measure of the average gain divided by the average loss. It is used to judge an individual market's strength on the basis of the average net change of candles or bars for a specified period and plots it in a range between 0 and 100. The formula for calculating RSI is

$$RSI = 100 - (100 / RS + 1)$$

where RS is average gain or average loss.

Welles Wilder, the developer of this indicator, recommended using 14 periods in calculating the average gain and average loss, and that is what we use. As the points are plotted, they oscillate between 0 and 100 and are commonly centered near the midpoint of 50. We concentrate on the midpoint, identifying an increase in momentum as the indicator passes through that level. An RSI reading below 50 reinforces a downtrend, and a reading above 50 supports an uptrend. Wilder also defined the RSI as an indicator to identify overbought or oversold conditions, keying on points above 70 as overbought and points below 30 as oversold. We respect his study by considering a cross down below 70 to be supportive of a sell trigger and a cross up above 30 to be supportive of a buy signal. It is rare to see an RSI reading above 80 or below 20, but when those numbers come, they are significant.

Figure 7-15 RSI 50 Cross Combined with Bull Trendline and Change-of-Direction Candles

A reading below 20 generally indicates that a lower low in price is still to come, and a reading above 80 almost always means that a higher high in price is to follow. RSI also is used in a similar manner to the other oscillators we have studied in that it can identify divergence between this indicator and price. Divergence would be supportive of a reversal or a countertrend trigger or signal. Figure 7-15 shows an example of why we key on the midpoint level (50) for this indicator.

In Figure 7-15 we can see from this 240-minute chart of USDJPY from early June 2008 that when the RSI closes above 50, we don't want to be anything but long. We see from the heavy black trendline below the market that we had a healthy up move in place and how the RSI gave us timely triggers in that the market proved us correct right away so that we did not have to sit through any kind of drawdown.

The RSI is also effective in identifying support and resistance in the market by monitoring the different levels of the RSI. Just as we can draw trendlines that act as support and resistance on the price chart, we can draw trendlines on an RSI chart that may act as support and resistance. By going back and studying the charts, you will find that often we will see the same levels proving support or resistance on the RSI, depending on the current trend. In a very strong market the RSI 50 level will prove support, as price will bottom at the same time the RSI finds support at this level. In a more modest up move price may bottom out when the RSI is at 40. In a downtrend we may see price start to top out when the RSI gets to around 60.

In Figure 7-16 we see how a resistance line for the RSI between 60 and 55 for the week of August 11 telegraphs a down move in EURUSD, whereas the support level angling up from approximately 30 to 35 a week later precludes an up move. The RSI is also effective at showing divergence, as can be seen in Figure 7-16, where the RSI bottoms on August 15 and then creates an uptrend before the price actually bottoms on August 19.

Just as the market respects the support and resistance levels created by isolated lows and highs, the RSI's isolated lows and highs become significant support and resistance levels and are well worth reviewing.

The RSI is an important indicator in that it is an excellent gauge of underlying strength as well as being an effective determinant of support and resistance independent of price points on the chart.

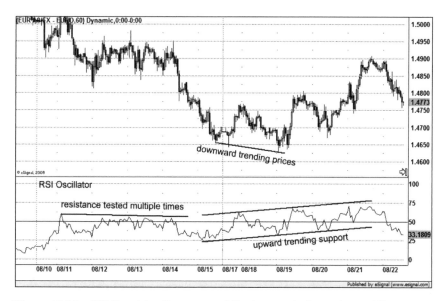

Figure 7-16 RSI Provides Support and Resistance Independent of Price

Commodity Channel Index

The Commodity Channel Index is a momentum oscillator that is considered a leading indicator. It was designed by Donald Lambert to identify cyclical turns in commodities. Lambert believed that commodities (or financial markets) move in cycles, with highs and lows coming at fairly regular intervals. The calculation involves taking the central pivot point of a market minus the 20-period simple moving average of that pivot point and dividing that number by 0.015 multiplied by the mean deviation. For our purposes, the calculation is not important, as the various chart packages do this for us; it is how the indicator is used that is noteworthy. Like all centered oscillators, the CCI fluctuates above and below a zero line.

Lambert's analysis concentrated on movements above 100 and below −100. What was noteworthy about Lambert's original calculation using a 0.015 constant was that it ensured that the majority of CCI values would fall between 100 and −100. When the market moves above 100, it is thought to be entering an uptrend and a buy signal is given, and when the market moves below the −100 CCI reading, a sell signal is generated. Similarly, a move up through −100 would be seen as a countertrend buy signal, whereas a move down though 100 would be seen as a countertrend sell signal. By not considering price action between the 100 and −100 levels, the trader avoids much of the sideways or countertrend price action and seeks out the times when markets enter into cyclical moves. It was also Lambert's belief that if a market has a statistical tendency toward a quarterly cycle—which would be approximately 60 trading days high to high or low to low—the CCI should be set to one-third of that, or 20 days. If a market has a six-month cycle, or 120 days, the CCI should be set to one-third of that, or 40 days. The CCI also can give signals generated from trendlines drawn on top of the indicator. As in all momentum oscillators, divergence between price and the CCI is considered significant as well. Figure 7-17 shows how a CCI trendline signal followed by a move above 100 provided timely buy signals in USDJPY. Assuming that a quarterly cycle is a good fit for a currency, we went with a 20 length CCI in this example.

The CCI is another versatile tool in the trader's toolbox in that it gives both trend and countertrend signals, attempts to filter out signals in ranging markets by concentrating on the 100 and -100 levels, gives us divergence, and allows us to draw trendlines on the indicator itself.

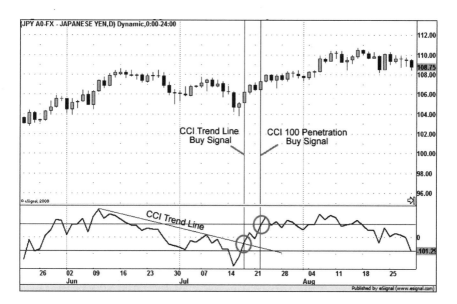

Figure 7-17 CCI Shows Its Versatility

Average True Range

The average true range (ATR) is not an indicator as much as it is a tool that gives us a market's average range over a specific period and accounts for price gaps from one day to the next or from one week to the next. Another word for what it is helping to measure is the market's current volatility, which is the rate of the change in price over time: The faster price is moving, the higher the volatility is, and the slower price is moving, the lower the volatility is. The indicator was developed by J. Welles Wilder and is one we can use to determine our stop placement, or how much we will risk on a trade. We cover stop placement orders in more detail in Chapter 12 but need to introduce you to this calculation and show you why and how we use it.

Figure 7-18 is a chart of EURUSD for the period from late 2008 to early 2009, with the ATR at the bottom of the chart. This indicator gives us the average true range for the previous 14 sessions. The reading on this chart for February 1 is 0.0237, which tells us that the ATR over the previous 14 sessions was 237 pips. Therefore, we can surmise that if we take a position in this market and want to place our stop far enough away from price to avoid being stopped out on a random intraday price spike, this information will be helpful. We may decide that a 2 ATR stop would be appropriate—placing our stop over 474 pips away from our entry—in that it would give us enough room to stay in the trade and not have to worry too much about price stopping us out prematurely. We are not recommending this as a strategy, just showing you how it can be used as one.

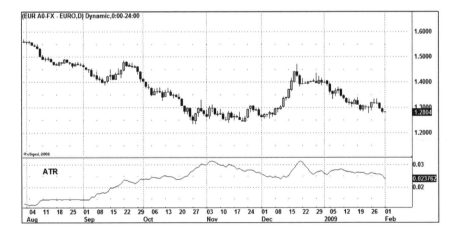

Figure 7-18 ATR Gives the Market's Current Average Range or Volatility

The ATR is helpful because we can judge at a glance how much a market is moving. That will help us determine how much we would need to expect to risk or if we could even afford to take a position in that market

In Chapter 9 we will cover ways to tie together the technical indicators we use, and in Chapter 13 you will see them again in a trading plan we've constructed that we encourage you to use as a model for your own trading plan.

CHAPTER 8

TRADING TECHNIQUES

Markets definitely have a cadence or a rhythm that a trader needs to tune in to. Often it's not enough to discern direction and look for signals until we've taken a moment to scan our longer-term charts for patterns in both price and time that a market may be exhibiting.

Time patterns play nearly as important a role in technical analysis as price patterns do but are talked about only rarely. When we refer to time patterns, we are not referring to market cycles such as those one might find in commodities or to sophisticated measurements based on Fibonacci ratios but to simple tendencies a market move may be exhibiting that can be seen easily on a chart and can give us an edge in our trading. Often a market will exhibit predictable behavior when it is correcting, as can be seen in Figure 8-1. The USDJPY fell into a pattern of taking 12-hour countertrend corrections that were easy to spot; the last one happened over the weekend

Figure 8-1   Pattern of 12-Hour Corrections in USDJPY

and so was a bit over the usual 12 hours, but it still was easy to spot.

Figure 8-2 shows a GBPUSD daily chart in which one can see a bull market that was exhibiting a tendency toward 10-week corrections and then 8-week corrections. Symmetry like this is common in most markets and is something experienced traders quickly home in on.

Figure 8-3 shows the EURJPY displaying a clear pattern of two-day corrections through June and July 2006. Time patterns such as these tend to show up in corrections (reactions) more than in trending (impulsive) markets, and that determination is in itself intuitive in that the timing of

Figure 8-2 Weekly Pattern to Corrections in GBPUSD

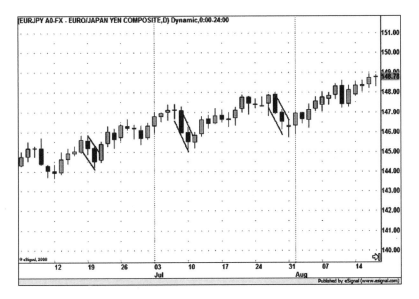

Figure 8-3 Simple Pattern of Two-Day Corrections

reactive behavior should be more predictable than that of impulsive behavior.

As quickly as markets show repetitive behavior, the pattern fades away and shows up at a later date with a slightly different cadence and a longer or shorter distance. Instead of trying to anticipate a pattern in market movement, it is far better to observe the market's current behavior and take the signals the market provides. "Take what the market gives you" is an old adage among traders, and for good reason.

It is important to remember that technical analysis is an art, not a science.

Dow Theory

Dow Theory is a trend-following school of thought named after Charles Dow, one of the original publishers of the *Wall Street Journal*, for his analysis of nineteenth-century market price action. The theory was refined by S. A. Nelson and William Hamilton and published by Robert Rhea in a book titled *The Dow Theory* in 1932. Hamilton's 1922 book *The Stock Market Barometer* is also a cornerstone of this theory.

Dow Theory covered trends extensively, breaking them down into three categories. The first is the primary trend, which lasts from a few months to many years and represents the dominant market direction: a bull or bear market. The primary trend is identified from the current direction of the peaks and troughs or pattern of highs and lows and closes on the daily or weekly charts. The trend is up if there is a series of higher highs, higher lows, and higher closes. The trend is down if there is a series of lower lows, lower highs, and lower closes. Primary moves also are characterized by relatively steady or impulsive movement in one direction.

The secondary trend is a price movement that can last from a few weeks to a few months and is defined as a corrective stage for a market when it deviates from its primary direction and retraces anywhere from one-third to two-thirds from the previous move. Secondary moves are characterized as reactive price actions and often are faster than primary moves. Hamilton considered secondary moves normal in the course of market movement and healthy in that they can offset excessive speculation.

Daily fluctuations, or the short-term trend, last from a few hours to a few days—rarely longer than a week—and represent very short-term reactions and corrections that often are brought about by fundamental developments or scheduled news releases.

In Robert Rhea's book, which is a partial compilation of Dow and Hamilton's original editorials, he laid out several assumptions that must be accepted if one intends to follow Dow Theory.

The first assumption is that the primary trend cannot be manipulated. In a widely followed liquid market such as a major stock index or a country's currency, manipulation over a long period is not possible. Even 100 years ago Dow and Hamilton felt that despite manipulations over the short term, major markets were too big to be controlled by anything other than the true underlying structure of supply and demand over the long term.

The second assumption is that markets discount everything. This means that the price the market is trading at represents all the information currently available regarding economic activity, interest rate levels, currency pricing, expectations of inflation, political developments, and product or commodity innovations. The unexpected can and will happen, but it generally will influence the very short-term or secondary trend, leaving the primary trend in place. This is a widely known tenet of technical analysis now, but it was groundbreaking when it was published at a time when the majority of investors pored over fundamental information in the previous day's newspapers for hints about what would happen in tomorrow's market.

The third assumption is that the theory is not perfect. It does not provide a way to outperform the averages every time but outlines a set of guidelines to assist traders in interpreting where a major market is in its cycle.

The theory also laid out rules for trend identification, using criteria such as a higher low in a downtrend followed by a higher high to confirm a trend change or reversal. This is considered common knowledge now among traders but serves as a reminder to beginning as well as experienced traders to pull up the long-term charts and always be aware of such developments and patterns.

The theory also is known for using one related average or market to confirm the action in another, closely connected average. A hundred years ago the two markets used were the Dow Jones Industrial Average and the Dow Jones Rails Average, the precursor to the Dow Jones Transportation Index. It was widely believed that the Rails Average would lead the Industrial Average because before industries could expand, they had to purchase and transport the raw materials needed for expansion. This early activity would show up in a railroad company's receipts before an increase in business activity for companies and businesses on the industrial side. Because of this relationship between industries, a move in one index generally had to be confirmed by a move in the other. Figure 8-4 is an example of this as we see the Dow Jones Industrial Average daily chart in disagreement with Dow Jones Transportation Index (the modern Rails Average) in the third quarter of 2008 as the Industrial Index makes a lower low and the Transportation Index does not. The market then goes sideways until the Transports make a lower low in late September 2008 and both indexes fall sharply in unison.

Figure 8-4 Transports Confirm Bear Market with Lower Low

This divergence between the two related indexes can tell us as traders that we do not want to press short positions in the Industrials until we have confirmation of a move lower in the Transports in the form of a lower low. Once the Transports confirmed with a lower low, we saw an acceleration of the down move by both indexes.

Dow Theory also breaks down market movement into three different stages. The first stage is marked by accumulation for a bull market or distribution for a bear market. This is followed by the middle stage, in which price movement accelerates as the fundamentals reinforce the price trend and price movement becomes impulsive. In the third stage there is exhaustive price action as rampant speculation kicks in and the market literally runs out of new participants because investors and speculators are all positioned the same way. These definitions are still helpful to market students and traders.

Hamilton and Dow covered volume and the way it lends validity to breakouts and trending behavior. They also covered sideways patterns, or what we've come to know as trading ranges. Much of what the theory covered evolved into the pattern-recognition techniques that we outlined in the section on chart patterns in Chapter 6.

A drawback of Dow Theory that is common to trend-following studies is that those systems are often late in confirming market movement. This leads investors to enter positions after a significant move already has taken place and leaves them to sit through adverse price corrections.

This section is meant to introduce Dow Theory, not define it. We encourage anyone with an interest in the theory to take an in-depth look at this school of thought by obtaining

Hamilton and Rhea's original works, which are available online. You will see after studying Rhea's *The Dow Theory* where some of the ideas for the next two schools of trading we are going to cover may have sprung from.

Elliott Wave

The Elliott wave principle is primarily a trend-following school of technical analysis that describes market movements as waves. In Elliot wave theory each market movement, or wave pattern, is designated with a numeric label—1 through 5—and a behavioral designation—impulsive (trending) or reactive (corrective). It is named after the market analyst R. N. Elliott, who published his ideas in two books: *The Wave Principle* (1938) and *Nature's Laws—The Secret of the Universe* (1946). Elliott wrote that a market movement, whether a bull move or a bear move, always could be broken down into five separate waves, with three being impulsive, or trending, moves and two being corrective, or countertrending, moves. The two corrective waves separated the three trending waves. The trending waves themselves could be broken down into five smaller waves of the same sequence as the overall move, and the corrective waves often fulfilled predictable retracements and broke down into three waves—two impulsive separated by one corrective—that are labeled A-B-C.

Elliott believed the Fibonacci summation series was the basis of his wave pattern. He theorized that it is crowd psychology that moves the markets, and since that was no more than the collective actions of individuals and since individuals, like all living things, are rhythmic, their actions can be predicted. He also proposed that there are waves within waves, with each smaller time frame mimicking the larger formation, a phenomenon we now know to be fractal geometry.

Figure 8-5 shows an example of a possible Elliott wave count on the daily USDJPY chart for the down move in 2007 and early 2008. We see three impulse moves down labeled 1, 3, and 5 and two corrective waves in between labeled 2 and 4 that show predictable retracements of approximately 50 percent and 66 percent. The move is symmetrical, with the impulse moves being roughly equal in height, lending predictability to the extensions, and with the corrective waves being marked by

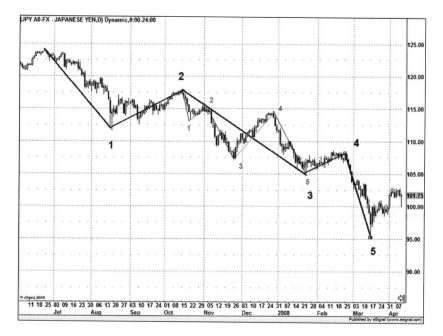

Figure 8-5   Elliot Wave Pattern in USDJPY

the choppy sideways price action common to countertrend or corrective price activity. Figure 8-5 also highlights one of the propositions of Elliott wave theory, which is that wave 3 is the most dynamic wave of the three impulse waves.

Figure 8-6 shows an example of a five-wave rally in the Dow Jones Industrial Average futures in 2007 followed by a textbook A-B-C correction. Note how wave 1 and wave 5 are nearly identical in size and how wave 3 is easily the largest and most dynamic. On the A-B-C correction that follows, the A wave is nearly identical to the C wave, continuing the symmetry of the up move it corrected.

According to his detractors, one of the drawbacks of Elliot's theories is that they are too subjective, with analysts needing

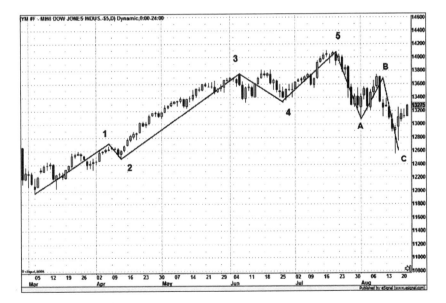

Figure 8-6 Elliot Wave in Dow Jones Industrial Average Index

to update and adjust their wave counts regularly as the market moves. Ellioticians seem to say that market direction is predetermined but then adjust their wave counts when the market doesn't play out the way they had scripted it to.

We feel that the trader and market forecaster Cynthia Kase summed it up best in her 1996 book *Trading with the Odds*: "Elliott's theories about the market in general and his view that there is a natural law that governs the market are correct in broad terms." The fact that traders such as Kase, along with Bill Williams and Justine Williams-Lara, the traders and authors of the *Trading Chaos* trilogy of books, continue to use the wave count in their trading also gives Elliott's theories credibility.

Our description of the Elliott wave here is relatively short considering the weight the theory carries with many professional traders. Elliott's wave theory and observations and use of Fibonacci numbers were groundbreaking, and there is no shortage of excellent descriptions of how his theories are applied in today's market, including Kase's works.

W. D. Gann

W. D. Gann is a name that many professional traders know well. Gann's 1942 book *How to Make Profits in Commodities* is a classic trading text that is full of sound advice covering topics from market trends, to isolated highs and lows, to swing trading, to volume analysis, to individual psychology and money management. Gann talked about the importance of studying the difference between a time period's opening price and closing price long before other analysts were talking about information that we now know is embodied in candlestick charts.

Despite his insistence on "never bucking the trend," Gann is best known for his countertrend theory that markets move in increments of one-eighths. He believed that if one took a completed market movement from top to bottom and divided it into eight equal sections and then extended those levels into the future, they would have predictive value. The levels would take turns providing both resistance and support, with the four-eighths, or 50 percent, level having particular significance in determining the trend. The three-eighths and five-eighths levels are also of particular importance in providing pivotal levels and determining the trend. When a market stalled at a Gann one-eighth level, it generally meant that market would retreat back to the previous level, and when a market closed through a Gann level, it meant it generally would continue its current direction to the next level. Gann also considered the seven-eighths level to constitute significant resistance and the one-eighth level to constitute significant support. Many of these occurrences can be seen in Figure 8-7. The Gann levels for this chart were anchored in 2000 when we measured the bear market of 1990 to 2000 and divided it into eighths and then extended those levels outward. Note the importance of the 50 percent level in 2003, 2004, and 2005 and the importance of 0.625 (five-eighths) in 2007 and 2008.

There were also 1.125 and 1.250 levels and −0.125 and −0.250 levels. According to the Gann expert T. Henning Murray, of Nashville, TN, once the market closed above 1.250

Figure 8-7 Monthly EURJPY Chart Broken Down into One-Eighth Gann Lines

(+2/8), the old 50 percent level (4/8) became the new 0.00 level (0/8) and the Gann lines shifted higher. Similarly, if price closed below −0.250 (−1/8), the old 50 percent level (4/8) became the new 1.00 (8/8) level and the Gann lines shifted lower. This shifting of the numbers gives the Gann lines a trend-following capability as they expand with the market.

Ironically, Gann's extension teachings on the benefits of trading with the trend, his theory of dividing market moves by 12.5, and his belief in the value of swing trading led many of his followers to concentrate on countertrend trading. The drawbacks to following Gann's tactics today come not from his original works but from the interpretations of those works by analysts and brokers trying to capitalize on Gann's name. Gann also was credited with using astrology in his analysis, largely as a result of his followers' interpretations. Gann also believed that fractal geometry was at work in the markets, with the distance between the larger one-eighth sections breaking down into smaller one-eighth sections.

Buying Strength and Selling Weakness

One of the most widely made mistakes by nonprofessional traders results from not understanding the concept of buying strength and selling weakness. Professional traders, in contrast, make a living by taking advantage of this concept. Let's say there were two currency markets in clearly defined downtrends. One market was higher by 0.58 percent on the day, and the other market was higher by 0.23 percent on the day. According to your methodology, both markets were giving sell signals, and you were instructed to choose between the two. Which market would you sell: the one up 0.58 percent or the one up 0.23 percent?

The correct answer is you would take the sell signal in the market that was up 0.23 percent because that was the weaker market. When we are given the choice, we always sell weakness and buy strength.

In the two charts in Figure 8-8, both AUDUSD and EURUSD are in extended downtrends. Both markets correct, or retrace, at the same time in late September 2008. We can see on the charts that AUDUSD retraced or rallied approximately 36 percent of the previous down move and EURUSD retraced or rallied approximately 46 percent of the down move. We can say that on the basis of the distance of this retracement, EURUSD is stronger than AUDUSD because it retraced more. When we get sell signals after the corrections in the form of price closing below short-term bull trendlines, AUDUSD falls over 10 percent and EURUSD falls only 5.6 percent. Clearly, we would have been well served by being short both pairs. However, we would have been better served—more profitable—by being short two AUDUSD rather than one of each.

To bring home to you how important it is to recognize weakness and strength and trade on this information, let's say that having seen how EURUSD was stronger than AUDUSD after that September correction, we decided to buy EURAUD at the

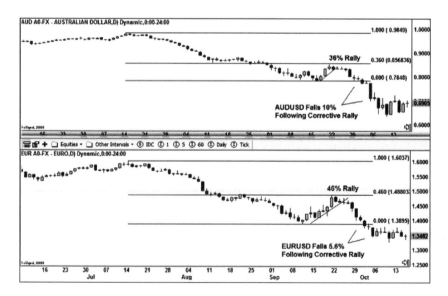

Figure 8-8 EURUSD Retraces More, Indicating That It Is the Stronger of the Two Markets

Figure 8-9 EURAUD Jumps Sharply in October 2008

end of September, based on the axiom of buying strength and selling weakness. Figure 8-9 shows the EURAUD chart.

This chart provides a great example of why professional traders always buy strength and sell weakness. The price corrections in September gave market participants a clear look at which markets were weaker than the others, and traders voted with their money, giving us a very impressive rally in EURAUD in early October.

Buying a currency that is lagging the other currencies relies on the same logic as betting on a horse that is in last place three-quarters of the way through the race for no other reason than that the horse is trailing. It makes no sense to initiate trades by buying a currency that is weak relative to the others or selling one that is strong relative to the others.

CHAPTER 9

TYING THE TECHNICAL INDICATORS TOGETHER: TRADE SIGNALS AND QUANTIFYING TRENDS

W ith technical analysis there is an order of operation to the technical indicators as a market swings from one direction to the next. The chart in Figure 9-1 provides an example of an order of operation that we can count on to play out nearly the same way across many different markets. Although some signals trigger first, leading us to emphasize them more initially, all the signals taken collectively are very powerful and lend predictive value to the analysis. Note again a market's tendency to migrate to the next higher time frame trendline once the shorter-term trendline is violated on a closing basis. Here is the collective order of operation for this case:

Individual candlestick behavior. We see a hammer with the body on the 1.0000 level.

Stochastic cross. The stochastic is a leading indicator and, when combined with the trendline violation, provides the first buy signal on this chart. The combination of the trendline break and the stochastic cross is definitely a signal to cover our short positions and for countertrend traders to initiate long positions. A countertrend signal would be defined as one in which the trend on the chart with the next higher time frame opposes the signal. When they are in a countertrend trade, traders are advised to monitor price action much more closely than they do in a trend trade. A trend trade is one in which the trend on the next higher time frame is in agreement with the signal. We will discuss this distinction later in this chapter.

Trendline break. When short-term two-point trendlines are updated properly, trendline violations are one of the first signals given on the chart before a change in direction. Trendline violations mean that the candle or bar closed through the trendline, and the first violation of the most recent trendline would be considered a countertrend signal.

Hammer to put in higher low. The higher low is the most important occurrence to date on the chart as it tells us the market is in fact exhibiting reversing behavior. The higher low implies that the market direction is shifting from lower to sideways. A close above the high of the hammer is also a buy signal. We will discuss this type of signal later in this chapter.

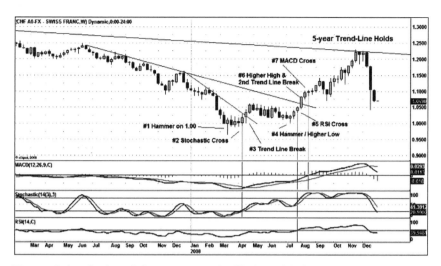

Figure 9-1 Order of Operation to the Technical Indicators

RSI 50 cross. An RSI cross above 50 is a buy signal that is always worth monitoring, but after a higher low, it is particularly significant. The market agrees, as we see USDCHF accelerate higher the next day.

Higher high and intermediate-term trendline violation. The higher high coming after the higher low indicates a trend shift. The market also closes above a bearish trendline here to start to shift the secondary trend (or intermediate-term trend) higher.

MACD zero line cross. The MACD is a lagging indicator, and when it crosses zero, it is a trend signal and generally confirms that the secondary, or intermediate, trend has shifted.

Figure 9-2 shows another example of the order of operation at work. The only difference in this example is that there was

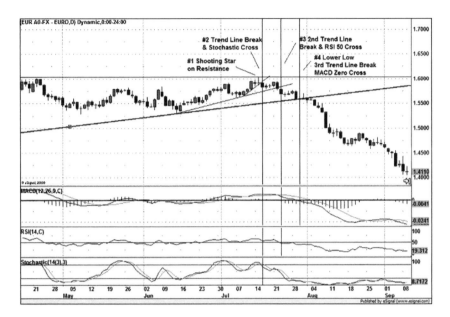

Figure 9-2 Technical Indicators and Trendlines

resistance in place in the form of the first peak of a double top. The order of the stochastic cross, with the RSI moving through 50 and the MACD crossing zero, remained the same, as did the trendline breaks from short-term to longer-term. Both examples also show the significance of technical signals given on the same bar, or candle, as trendline breaks.

Detractors of technical indicators point to the fact that they work only half the time at best. It is true that we never would want to trade strictly off the technical indicators, and there is a reason why we covered charts, support and resistance, trendlines, and chart patterns before discussing technical indicators. Technical indicators, however, play a key role in our trading as they help us identify the stage of a trend we are in.

The stochastic cross is paramount in determining the short-term, or micro, trend, and the MACD zero line cross often gives us the intermediate, or secondary, trend. Technical indicators reinforce what market direction is telling us and play a role in giving a trader confidence.

It's reasonable for a trader to have more confidence in initiating a short position in a mature downtrend when the RSI is below 50 and the MACD is below the zero with little or no divergence on the time frame she or he is trading. If a market has been in a sustained uptrend, exhibiting double or triple divergence, we may pass on the buy signal. Even for the most experienced traders, divergence and momentum are difficult to spot without the aid of the technical indicators. When one is trading multiple markets while coordinating multiple time frames, the technical indicators come in handy in helping one keep direction in perspective. Rather than looking back over past activity to discern a trend, it is often far easier to glance at the MACD and see in an instant that it has closed definitively above or below the zero line.

Similarly, we can see at a glance how the stochastic is positioned, and that helps us identify the short-term trend. Figure 9-3 shows a good example of this. The trendlines don't help us here, as it looks like price is going into a symmetrical triangle. The technical indicators, however, give us a heads-up that this market is in fact primed for a 100-pip-plus sell-off. The technical indicators on one time frame also give us insight into the trends unfolding on the next lower time frame by reason of time. If the stochastic and the current trendline are telling us that the short-term trend is shifting higher on the daily chart, they also are telling us that the secondary trend on the 240-minute chart is

Figure 9-3   Technical Indicators Identify Market Weakness

shifting higher, and this is essential information for swing traders and intraday traders.

Figure 9-4 provides an example of how the technical indicators can keep us from taking a losing trade or at least tell us
that an uptrend needs to be watched closely for signs of a correction, or reversal. The trend is up, yet both the MACD and
the RSI are telling us that momentum has fallen off, indicating
that we should take a pass on the buy signal created by the
short-term trendline violation on August 12.

All the overlays and indicators, as well as all the support and
resistance levels we've looked at, are tools that help us gauge
a market's current direction and momentum. This helps us
move along with the market instead of trying to guess what
the market will do next. Any individual tool can do only the

Figure 9-4   Technical Indicators Help Identify a Trend Shift

job it was designed to do. Taken collectively, however, these tools are very powerful and will help us understand market direction and help define our choices as traders. You should be starting to get a grasp of price behavior and direction on an individual chart. The next step is to tie price behavior together by using multiple time frames and charts.

Trade Signals

Each of the technical indicators or studies we reviewed earlier gives us a trade signal in some form. We respect them all, particularly when they occur on existing support or resistance and/or are in the same direction as the current trend. One of the most reliable trade signals is the combination trendline break and stochastic cross. In the last section we talked about what happens when a trend reverses and how the order of operation for the technical indicators plays out. Right at the top of the list was the trendline break and the stochastic cross. The combination of these two occurrences is always noteworthy because a shift in the trend cannot occur without them. Because of the simplicity and reliability of this signal, it is one of the first trade signals we will be covering.

We see an example of these signals in Figure 9-5, where we have the signals marked by vertical lines that show the candles that gave us the signals. The vertical line on the left side of the

Figure 9-5 Combination Stochastic and Trendline Trade Signal

chart marks a sell signal given by the combination of the price closing below a short-term up trendline and the stochastic crossing below the oversold line. The vertical line on the right marks a buy signal marked by a close above the bear trendline combined with the stochastic moving higher above the oversold line. The trendline drawn is intermediate-term in length as it is between 15 and 60 candles.

Also note how the MACD supports both the sell signal and the buy signal. To take a sell signal, we prefer to see that the MACD histogram has stair-stepped lower at least once, which tells us that there is a shift in momentum in favor of the signal. For the buy signal on the right side of the chart, we see that although MACD is below zero, the MACD histogram is stair-stepping in the direction of the trigger.

When we use the trendline and stochastic cross signal, we don't need the MACD histogram for confirmation, but we want it to confirm within the next couple of candles. A rule of thumb is that if we are considering a trade signal and the MACD histogram is moving opposite to the signal, we know we are very likely to be entering a countertrend trade and should be even more active in monitoring the trade. Preferably, we want at least the MACD histogram starting to stair-step in favor of the trade.

Figure 9-6 provides two more examples of trade signals given by the trendline and stochastic combination. In the first case the MACD does not confirm, and in the second it does.

For the first buy signal on the left side of the chart in Figure 9-6, we see that the signal did help identify a bottom, but the trader would have had to sit through a drawdown on his or her position and a retest of that low. The reason for this

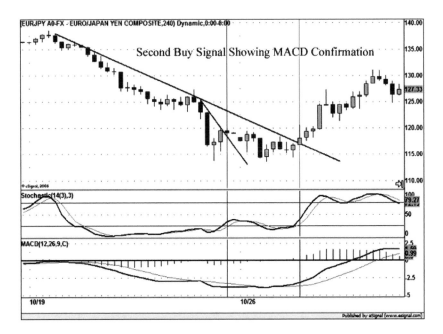

Figure 9-6 MACD Confirms Trade Signal

is that the momentum of the down move was too strong, as marked by the increased slope of the sell-off. When we see momentum that strong before a signal, we may decide that it does not warrant the risk of taking the trade. When a price move is marked by a nearly parabolic candle like this one, it is best to stick with signals in the same direction as the momentum or just not trade. The MACD confirms our decision not to take the signal as it is below both the zero line and the trigger line. Eventually the market gave us a rounded bottom, and the next buy signal on the right side of the chart provided a nice trade as the intermediate-term trendline was penetrated. At the time of this signal the MACD confirmed by crossing above the trigger line to give us a countertrend buy signal.

The next signal we are going to cover is a close above a bullish doji and a close below a bearish doji. When the market gives us a doji or, more specifically, a shooting star doji at or near resistance and then has a close below the low of that doji, this is a sell signal. The shooting star candle tells us the market is indecisive, and the candle that closes below that low would be a change-of-direction candle by definition because it closes below the low of the doji. We can take this combination of candles as a sell trigger.

On the October 2008 GBPJPY chart shown in Figure 9-7 we see a pair of sell signals created by a shooting star dojis followed immediately by change-of-direction candles that closed below the low of the dojis. The change-of-direction candle is often going to provide a signal because by definition

Figure 9-7 Candlestick Trade Signals

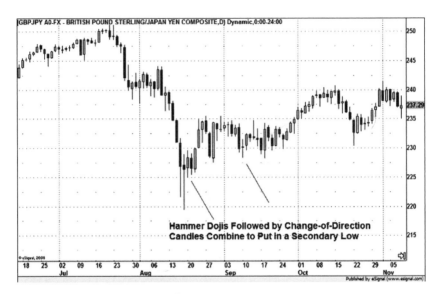

Figure 9-8 Candlestick Buy Signals

it is breaking the previous pattern of price action, and it also is very likely to create a short-term trendline break. In her 1996 book *Trading with the Odds,* Cynthia Kase describes how she often uses this signal to exit trades.

Figure 9-8 shows examples of hammer dojis followed by change-of-direction candles in the summer of 2007 that marked a secondary low in GBPJPY.

Trending and Countertrending Behavior

In Chapter 4 we touched on the difference between trending and countertrending markets by pointing out that elongated candles extending up or down identify trending, or impulsive price action, whereas shorter candles with smaller bodies indicate countertrending price action, or reactive trading. This is an important distinction for a trader because although our indicators and overlays remain the same, our trading strategy will differ slightly with the type of market we are in. A trending market is one in which the directional bias is obvious and can be seen on the chart by a pattern of highs, lows, and closes moving in the same direction. A countertrending market is one in which there is no obvious direction other than sideways. Trending markets call for making quick decisions upon entering a trade but showing more patience once one is in the market, whereas countertrending markets give the trader more time in taking a trade but require less time in the trade and speed in exiting. Trending markets by definition are impulsive and move easily in one direction, whereas countertrend markets are reactive by nature and exhibit indecisive price action. We can define a trend trade as a position taken in the same direction as the overall pattern of highs, lows, and closing prices. A countertrend trade is one in which the trader is going against, or fading, the overall direction of the market in anticipation of a correction or a reversal or a trade in which the objective is to take advantage of a sideways market by selling near the top of the current price range and buying near the bottom.

Beginning traders often are attracted to countertrend trading because of the perceived level of risk. To someone with a small account, buying a market at a support level after a sharp price drop and then placing a tight stop-loss order can seem like a better choice than waiting for a market to correct or retrace and then turn before entering the trade and then placing a stop-loss order some distance away, below the last swing high. We believe a trader is better off recognizing the environment she is in by seeing the overall pattern of highs and lows and gauging the momentum before making the decision to go with a trending strategy in which once she is in the trade, she may use a lagging indicator and plan to allow the trend to develop. Or a trader can decide to employ a countertrend strategy in which he uses support and resistance, individual candle behavior, and/or a leading indicator to get in and out of trades faster. In the long run, trend traders will be rewarded more because they will be taking advantage of the market's tendency to trend. Countertrend trading strategies can be successful but require more diligence and create higher transaction costs because of the higher frequency of trading.

To enter any trade, whether in a trending or a countertrending environment, we generally prefer to use a signal generated by a leading indicator coupled with a short-term trendline break. In a countertrending environment, though, we can speed up our entry process by using the closing price beyond a doji or inside candles on existing support or resistance as the trigger. In countertrending markets we want to get in our position as close to the top or bottom of the range as we can. In a trending environment, in contrast, we want the market to give us more of an indication that it is turning rather than just a pause in support or resistance. In a strong trending market it is best to pass on countertrending signals unless you have the time and skill to trade on a lower time frame.

Something to know and remember about markets is that they exhibit fractal geometry. What this means is that price behavior on the higher time frames is mimicked by price behavior on the lower time frames. If we are seeing pronounced trending behavior on the daily chart, we can expect trending behavior on the intraday charts. This does not mean that the intraday movement will always be in the same direction as the primary trend; it means that the candles will be longer, which can seem counterintuitive to untrained traders. Similarly, if the market is in a narrow sideways range over an extended period on the daily chart, we would expect similar reactive behavior on an intraday basis.

A very important difference between a trending market and a countertrending market is that in a trending market the higher time frames will dictate price movement and direction, whereas in a countertrending environment the lower time frame charts can dictate direction. This means that in a trending market you do not want to go against the trend on the next higher time frame. In a countertrending market you are taking signals on the lower time frames routinely regardless of the previous direction on the higher time frames.

We titled this section "Trending and Countertrending Behavior" instead of "Trending versus Countertrending Behavior" because to be a complete trader, you must do both. The easiest way to define whether you are in a trending or a countertrending market is to define the trends on the different time frames and see if they are in agreement, which would mean a trending market, or are conflicting, which would mean a countertrending market. We are going to teach you how to do that in the next section.

Higher Time Frame Confirmation and Quantifying the Trend

In this section we consider the words *intermediate* and *secondary*, with the words *long-term* and *primary* interchangeable. We generally refer to a market movement as secondary and describe the trend that constitutes that movement to be intermediate-term. Similarly, we measure a primary move by identifying the long-term trend.

Knowing how to use a higher time frame chart to confirm a price signal on a lower time frame is a skill that can reward a trader greatly. Many students will become impatient and take a trade that is coordinated on the lower time frames, not on the higher time frames. This is a mistake and often a waste of time, energy, and, more important, money. Although you may not always have all the time frames line up, there will be times when this happens. More often than not, though, if you are trading an intraday chart and have the current trend on the daily chart lined up in the same direction, you are going to have the wind at your back. If you have the knowledge to identify markets in which the intraday trends are moving in the same direction as the daily and weekly trends, you are going to put yourself in a position to reap a reward.

Here are the time frames we analyze and trade from:

Monthly ← → weekly ← → daily ← → 240 minutes ← →
60 minutes ← → 15 minutes ← → 5 minutes

The different time frames we use must remain three to six increments apart to maintain continuity:

Monthly/4 = weekly chart
Weekly/5 = daily chart
Daily/6 = 240-minute chart
240/4 = 60-minute chart
60/4 = 15-minute chart
15/3 = 5-minute chart

In analyzing a market we never skip over a time frame. If we are trading off a 60-minute chart, we look to our 240-minute chart for confirmation. We never jump time frames because we would lose continuity. If we see a signal on the daily chart, we look to the trend on the weekly chart for confirmation. If we see a signal or setup on the 15-minute chart, we look to the 60-minute chart for confirmation. It is paramount to maintain this continuity.

The collage of charts in Figure 9-9, with the long-term on the left, the intermediate-term on the lower right, and the short-term on the upper right, provides an excellent perspective from which to analyze and trade markets. (For this example we are using the monthly chart for the long term, the weekly chart for the intermediate term, and the daily chart for the short term.) Here we see the market's stance, with the higher time frame charts encompassing all the activity on the lower time frame charts. We've overlaid most of the significant support and resistance levels and trendlines on the charts, along with the MACD, stochastic, and RSI at the bottom. (For ease of viewing we have omitted the RSI on the lower time frame charts.) We should always take direction and identify a trade setup from our intermediate-term chart, in this case the weekly chart. We can look to the long-term chart for confirmation or support—though this is not a prerequisite, particularly if one is day trading—and use the short-term chart to hasten our entry and exit signals.

Figure 9-9 Coordinating Time Frames

In Figure 9-9 we can see from price action and from the MACD being below zero on the monthly chart that the current trend is lower. We've marked the weekly chart with two vertical lines to show both the close of the week when the stochastic crossed its trigger line and the oversold line at 75 and the period when the bull trendline from March 2008 through August 2008 was penetrated on a closing basis. We've also marked the corresponding periods when those events occurred on the monthly chart and the daily chart with vertical lines. For the monthly chart there is only one line as both of those events occurred in one month. Note also on the monthly chart that when this market topped out just above 110.00, it gave us a

222

shooting star doji followed by a change-of-direction candle that closed below the low of the doji. This is certainly a bearish development, but we do not have penetration of the five-month bull trendline. Looking again to the weekly chart, we can see the advantage of waiting for sell indications on our intermediate-term chart to initiate positions on our daily chart. Traders who take signals from the daily chart without waiting for confirmation on the weekly chart risk getting into positions prematurely, and traders who wait for confirmation on the monthly chart risk missing the move and getting into the trade too late. Waiting for the weekly chart to confirm does not necessarily mean waiting till the end of the week. If the behavior of price on the weekly chart gives us a sell indication on a daily close, we can take this as higher time frame confirmation.

As a general rule we look first to a market for a tradable setup on its intermediate-term time frame. If we see an attractive setup such as the beginnings of a trend shift following price challenging a confluence of a long-term trendline and a Fibonacci level, we would look to our long-term time frame for confirmation. The trend on the long-term chart does not have to be in the same direction as the shift on the intermediate-term chart but should be showing behavior that indicates that it is shifting, such as a stochastic cross or MACD histogram shift or a close beyond a doji on support or resistance in the direction of the shift on the intermediate-term chart. If we have a favorable setup on the intermediate-term chart, we can wait to take a signal on that chart or look to the short-term chart for a signal in the same direction. If we take a signal on the short-term chart and the intermediate-term chart doesn't confirm within three candles, we need to exit the trade quickly.

We always place our charts on the screen (the computer monitor) in this order for a reason: The trader's eye should fall on the intermediate-term chart first. If direction is not obvious, we change to another market and keep doing that until we find one with obvious direction. Once we find a market with a favorable setup on the intermediate-term chart, based on support and resistance, trend, and current candlestick behavior, we monitor the shorter-term chart for a trade signal. By placing the different time frame charts on our screens in the same manner every time, we train ourselves always to look to the same area of the screen for the same information. You will find this repetition both comfortable and reliable. After you have viewed hundreds and then thousands of screen shots in this manner, your intuition will be drawn into your analysis and trading.

There is a difference between analyzing a market and trading a market. From a trading perspective, for all but the most experienced (well-capitalized) and confident traders, it is not realistic to put yourself in a position where you have to wait for the monthly chart to complete before exiting a position. It's preferable to start out by seeing the big picture and having existing trends in place that are in agreement with your position. The markets, however, are very dynamic pricing vehicles, and when underlying shifts occur, they do so quickly. "Change happens" is something experienced traders don't need to be told. Because of this there are time frames we analyze the market from, such as monthly-weekly-daily, and time frames we trade the market from, such as the weekly-daily-240-minute, 240-minute-60-minute-15-minute, or even 15-minute and 5-minute. In moving from analyzing a market to trading a market, our measurements for trends such as short-term, intermediate-term, and long-term also are adjusted. For trading, we define the three time frames as the short-term trend, which can be as short as two candles if price has closed beyond the last trendline and as long as 15 candles; the secondary trend, which can be as long as 15 to 60 candles; and the primary trend, which can be from 60 candles to hundreds. It's also important to understand that on any one chart there are these three time frames or trends at play. On the 60-minute chart there would be a short-term trend, an intermediate-term trend, and a long-term term at play, as there would be on the 240-minute chart and the daily chart. On the 240-minute GBPUSD chart shown in Figure 9-10 we have identified these three trends.

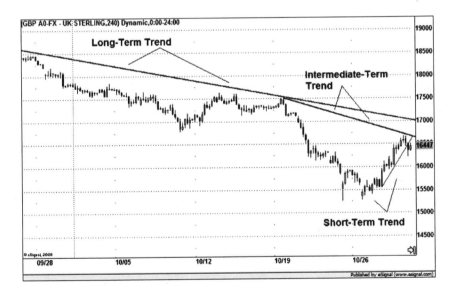

Figure 9-10 Trendlines Quantified

Another way to determine the short-term trend, aside from noting the pattern of the most recent highs, lows, and closes and trendlines, is by using the direction of the stochastics.

Figure 9-11 shows how tightly the stochastic follows the short-term trendline shifts and how the shifts occur as old trendlines give out, allowing a new trendline to begin. A good rule of thumb for active markets is that once the stochastics cross and close above the oversold line, the short-term trend has shifted higher, and once they cross and close below the oversold line, the short-term trend has shifted lower. As always, we need to confirm the trend by the pattern of highs, lows, and closes. Another technical rule of thumb is that once the MACD crosses and closes above or below zero, the intermediate-term trend is shifting.

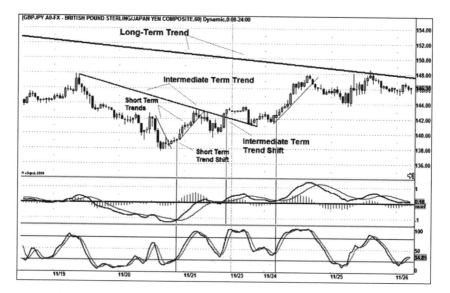

Figure 9-11 Using the Technical Indicators to Quantify Trend

Being patient and observing how the different trendlines shift like this will give you confidence and help you understand how price action works. Knowing the various trends at work in the market also helps a trader coordinate lower time frame charts. If the short-term and intermediate-term trends are higher on the 240-minute chart, we don't have to look to know that it is very likely that the primary trend on the 60-minute chart also will be higher. If the intermediate-term trend is higher on the 240-minute chart, most likely the short-term trend on the daily chart will be higher. The implications of this are very important for traders on both the lower and higher time frames. Knowing when the trends started and in which direction they are pointed is also a simple way to determine whether the market we are analyzing is in a trending or countertrending mode. If the majority of trends, particularly the long-term trends, are pointing in the same direction, we are in a trending market. If the trends are in flux, we are very likely in a countertrend market.

It is also important to understand that once a short-term trendline is violated, it is likely that the market will migrate to the intermediate-term trendline, and once the intermediate-term trend is violated, it becomes more likely that the market will try to test the long-term trendline. It is often at this point, after a closing penetration of the intermediate-term trend, that a market will show us whether it has real underlying strength or this is just another secondary move. Note in Figure 9-11 how powerful the stochastic buy signal marked by the gray vertical line on November 24 turned out to be. This was the case because we already had an intermediate-term trend shift in place. This short-term stochastic signal was the equivalent of two streams meeting and forming a river. The short-term buy signal confirmed the intermediate-term trend shift, and the market accelerated higher before being stopped by the force of the resistance powered by the long-term, or primary, trend.

When we view our charts, we always want the proper amount of time visible to use in making our decisions. The preferred amount of time is as follows:

Monthly chart	= 7 years
Weekly chart	= 2.5 years
Daily chart	= 8 months
240-minute chart	= 1.5 months
60-minute chart	= 10 days
15-minute chart	= 28 hours
5-minute chart	= 8 hours

Higher Time Frame Confirmation

In Figure 9-12 we see a trend trade setup for trading the USDCHF market; both charts are for the same market but on different time frames. We would be looking for the setup and signal on the chart on top, in this case the daily chart, and using the next higher time frame chart, the weekly, on the bottom to confirm.

In light of the sell-off in mid-September and the subsequent buy signal in late September by the stochastic indicator on the daily chart—see the vertical line on both charts—this would be an attractive buy setup. Although the short-term trend is lower here on the daily chart, both the secondary trend and the primary trend remain higher. Despite a falling stochastic on the

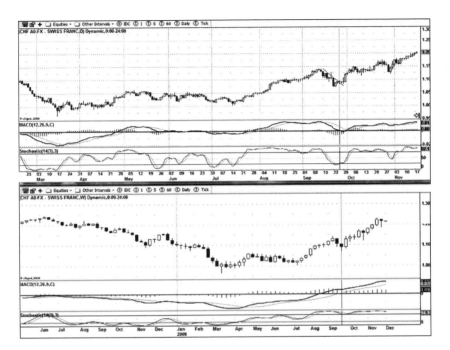

Figure 9-12   Higher Time Frame Confirmation

weekly chart, the short-term trend here also remains higher, with the same stochastic remaining above the overbought line at the 75 level. This setup makes for an acceptable risk-reward ratio. We can buy on the stochastic signal on the daily chart with a stop-loss order beneath the last swing low for an approximate two-point loss. Seven sessions after the buy signal, the market had risen by six points. Before this trade we also can see from the recent price action on the daily chart that after a steady two-month up move, perhaps this market is due for a correction. Remember that in Chapter 5 we talked about how seasoned traders know to expect corrections and understand that they are a healthy part of directional moves. That is a good lesson to keep in mind. A steady rally is an indication of market strength, particularly when there is no obvious resistance above the market. A price correction, or sell-off, in such a market can provide a buying opportunity more easily than an actual price reversal can.

We also must address how impulsive price movement—candles of the same color with elongated bodies—and countertrending price movement—shorter-candles of different colors with dojis—will differ depending on which stage a market is in on the higher time frame charts. Although it can be counter to the primary trend, a secondary trend often starts as an impulsive price move. It is this impulsive, or trending, behavior defined by elongated candles that leads traders to think that a new trend has developed when what actually has happened is that a short-term trendline has given way and the market is moving to test the next level of support or resistance.

Figure 9-12 provides a good example of this price behavior. Bear market rallies and bull market corrections are also examples of this. When a bear market gives us a countertrend or secondary rally, it generally occurs as long-term traders cover their short positions and shorter-term traders initiate long positions to take advantage of a quick move. The speed and strength of this move, particularly after a drawn-out move, lead inexperienced and shorter-term traders to believe that a reversal has occurred. Unlike long-term trends, which build strength slowly over time before climaxing with wide price ranges and heavy volume, secondary moves that prove to be countertrend corrections of the overall long-term trend start out fast and strong, exhibiting impulsive behavior, before fading quickly as price extends itself back up or down until it runs into the force of the primary trend. These secondary moves are a healthy way for the market to let off steam after the primary trend overextends itself.

These price corrections can be particularly tricky when they come after an actual reversal of a primary bull trend, when many market participants believe the previous trend is still intact. They believe they are seeing an opportunity to initiate longs in the direction of the overall trend but then get caught in the second down leg of a new primary move. Similarly, when an extended bear market gives way to a new bull market, inexperienced or shorter-term traders can get caught selling into the sell-off that follows the first rally after an actual reversal, only to see price move against their position in the same direction as the new primary trend. Thus, we need to understand that impulsive or trending price behavior also can occur counter to the primary trend.

Figure 9-13 shows an example of a bear market rally, or a secondary move counter to the primary downtrend, in the EURJPY in October 2008. Note that on the 240-minute chart on the left we can see price making lower lows during the week starting October 5; however, we also see positive divergence building as both the MACD and the stochastic record higher lows in this week. This provides a good heads-up that the odds of a countertrend move are increasing, particularly as prices continues to angle away from the long-term and intermediate-term bear trendlines as the primary trend extends itself. The divergence on the 240-minute chart is indeed a harbinger of a secondary rally as price closes above the short-term trendline on October 10 and the intermediate-term trendline on October 13. After the close above the intermediate-term bear trendline we see impulsive price action as the market sprints higher. At this point it is tricky to determine whether we have a new trend in place or simply a secondary rally just before a climax. As long as we are below the long-term trendline, we assume the second case: We are seeing a secondary rally marked by impulsive price behavior that tends to fade quickly in the face of the more mature primary trend. Note how the last candle on the 240-minute chart on the left would make it look to the untrained eye that EURJPY is in a good position to move higher and test the long-term trendline just below 145.00, having just made a higher high to close above the previous week's high. The long-term trendline above the price, however, provides a reminder of which way the primary trend still is pointed.

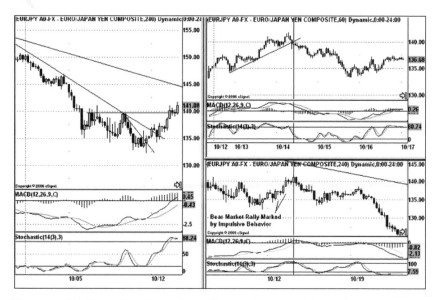

Figure 9-13 Identifying Secondary Moves

The chart on the lower right in this figure is also a 240-minute chart. We've placed a vertical line on this chart to mark the candle that was the last candle in the larger chart on the left. That candle marked the top of the countertrend, or secondary move. The point here is that it is wise to keep track of the primary trend and the secondary trend because by nature a secondary move will start out strong and fast but fade sooner than inexperienced traders think, just as the primary trend will start slower yet stay intact longer and move farther than most market participants think. Another word of caution about secondary moves: Because they start out fast and exhibit impulsive behavior, they generally will overrun support and resistance levels such as previous highs and lows, pivots, and retracement levels quickly, leaving untrained traders to believe that a new trend is under way.

Continuing with our example in Figure 9-13, we now look at the 60-minute chart on the upper right. Note that there is a vertical line on this chart marking the same time interval that is on the 240-minute chart below it. We should start to understand now that when we get a sell signal here in the form of a trendline break and a stochastic cross, although it would be a countertrend to the secondary move under way on the 240-minute chart, it is in the same direction as the primary trend on the chart with the higher time frame. These are favorable setups because most of the shorter-term momentum traders are positioned for a resumption of the current intermediate-term rally or secondary move that follows the market's higher high, believing there is room above for it to continue to rally. We may be long ourselves, having taken the countertrend buy signal on the 240-minute or 60-minute chart that marked the beginning of the secondary move. Once we saw the divergence on the 60-minute chart given by both the MACD and the stochastic, followed by the sell signal, we would exit our countertrend longs and swing short, back in the direction of the primary trend.

There are a couple of lessons in this example. First, we need to know that as traders risking our hard-earned money in the marketplace, we have to have the freedom to drop down to lower time frames to maximize our performance and still follow our trading plan. Similarly, we need the ability to trade higher time frames to catch primary trends with the same trading plan. As you see in the charts in this section, we are doing just that, and we are using the same overlays and indicators.

Coordinating time frames also means seeing setups on a higher time frame and then waiting for a signal in the same direction on the next lower time frame. An important aspect of this tactic is to remember that once the signal comes on the lower time frame, it is important to look back to the higher time frame to make sure the indications that originally warranted the signal are still in place. Figure 9-14 shows a sustained downtrend in EURJPY on the 240-minute chart in the lower panel, with the MACD well below the zero line. The chart on top is a 60-minute chart of the same market over the same period. Note that to the left of the vertical lines, starting on September 5, 2008, and running through September 9, 2008, we see a sharp rally. We would draw our support trendlines underneath this rally and wait for a penetration on a closing basis to give us a sell signal on the 60-minute chart on top. Once we get a sell signal, we check back to our 240-minute chart and see that it is still below its primary bear trendline and that the MACD is still below zero. This confirms the sell trigger. With the MACD being

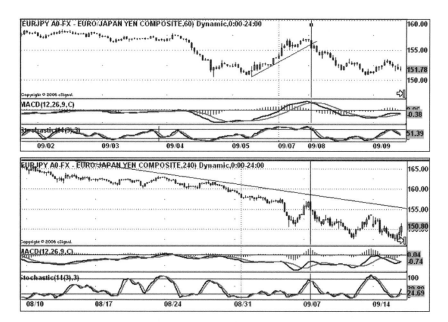

Figure 9-14 Intraday Higher Time Frame Confirmation

below zero on the 240-minute chart, we have assurance that the primary trend on the 60-minute chart is lower. We also would place a buy stop-loss order in the marketplace just beyond the bear trendline on the 240-minute chart; less capitalized traders could place the buy stop-loss order above the high of September 7.

When we see a trade signal on a chart and look to the next higher time frame for confirmation, it does not mean that the trend must be in agreement, but it does mean we should be seeing indications that support the signal in the lower time frame. An indication on the higher time frame that is in agreement with the lower time frame could be considered a countertrend signal by a leading indicator such as a stochastic trigger line cross, divergence on a momentum indicator, a trendline violation, or even a one-bar reversal on the MACD histogram.

Figure 9-15 shows an example of a primary trend reversal and how we needed to analyze the monthly and weekly charts to confirm this sea change occurrence. Keep in mind that primary trend reversals are rare and that a trader or market student will see many more continuation patterns than reversal patterns in his or her career.

In Figure 9-15 we see GBPUSD give us a sell signal on the weekly chart (top chart) in the form of a trendline break and a stochastic cross, with the monthly chart (bottom chart) confirming.

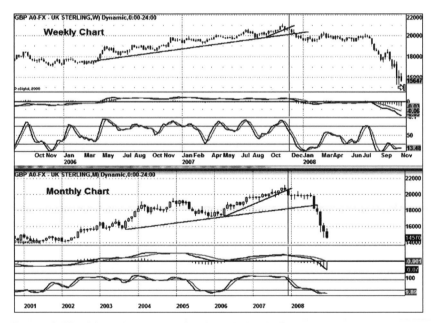

Figure 9-15 Monthly Activity Confirms Weekly Figure

The premise of coordinating time frames is to use the higher time frame to confirm the signal on the time frame we are trading. It is also important that we see that what generally is a countertrend signal on a short-term or intermediate-term chart can be a trend signal on a longer-term chart. This happens often and is something we can look for by always being aware of trade setups in close proximity to our primary trendlines. It is in these areas that secondary moves often weaken and show negative divergence before the market resumes its primary direction.

The downside of using higher time frame charts to confirm lower time frame charts comes when we are in a sideways or countertrending market or when we are seeing trends reversing. If we always use the higher time frame to confirm, we will miss the reversals, which by definition occur on the lowest time frames first. This is why it is so important that traders understand the importance of both trend trading and countertrend trading. Swing traders, who take every signal regardless of trend, know the advantage of both trend and countertrend trading because they know that by taking every trade they are assured of not missing the more powerful ones, which reversal trades, like established trend trades, tend to be. We cover swing trading in Chapter 11.

Despite all the trending price action in the forex markets over the last several years and the currency market's reputation for trending behavior compared with other markets, the norm for these markets and most financial markets is that they move sideways more often then they trend. Professional traders know this, and that is why so many of them are market makers and short-term scalpers who don't trade direction at all, at least not on a regular basis. Many inexperienced traders don't understand what it means to trade without a directional bias, but the pros do. The forex dealers who take the other side of retail traders' positions understand that markets move up and down and that by having just a pip or a couple of pips of advantage on every trade they take, they can make a lot of money on a day-to-day basis by taking the other side of their customers' trades and offsetting those positions at a slight profit or breakeven as the markets ebb and flow. Professional traders far more often than not do not care about direction. They already have their methods and systems in place. They care only about execution. The danger in knowing this for most market students is that they try to emulate the professional's short-term time horizon but don't have the professional's built-in advantages that arise from long-term back testing, institutional price feeds, and a well-capitalized account size.

Another big problem for many beginning and undercapitalized traders is that they spent too much time trying to figure out which direction they think the market will move in on the lower time frames instead of just taking signals and moving in whichever direction the market moves. One way to bypass this problem of "analysis paralysis" is to back test or demo trade a swing trading method in which the trader is not concerned about directional bias and concentrates only on execution. When we give complementary Webinars, we almost always demonstrate a signal or method that does not rely on directional bias because we know that most beginners fall into the trap of trying to figure out direction instead of concentrating on and learning execution. Instead, we encourage beginning traders to be patient and wait for trend setups when they trade real money. To give them the maximum amount of experience before they get to that point and to help them learn how markets ebb and flow, we teach our students how to trade a market from both sides.

Figure 9-16 shows a 60-minute chart of EURJPY. We chose this market to demonstrate trading both sides because it was late in the year—the beginning of December—and after a major move down from midsummer, this market had posted a low in October, which had held again in November, and the momentum indicators on the daily chart were showing positive divergence. That information told us that we had a market that probably was pausing, making it a good target for countertrend trading. We marked the November low with the heavy black horizontal support line on the chart and keyed off that to take buy signals and let the market, through the stochastic and trendline violations, tell us where to enter, exit, and

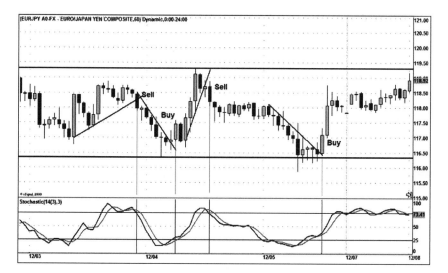

Figure 9-16 Combination Trendline Violation with Stochastic Cross Signal

reverse. Once a possible trading range was established, we marked the upper limit with another heavy black horizontal line. The signals are marked by a vertical gray line extending up from the stochastic cross to the candle that violated the trendline on a closing basis. By still taking sell signals, we had the benefit of taking trend trades, as the primary trend on the daily chart was still lower. However, if the market reversed and we saw a secondary rally, we stood a good chance of benefiting from that also as we were taking countertrend buy signals.

The method shown in Figure 9-16 should be familiar to you now because it uses the first signal we taught you earlier: the combination trendline violation–stochastic cross signal. This may seem to be a very simple signal, and it is. Most professional programmers familiar with the myriad trading systems in the marketplace today will tell you that the more simple the system, meaning the fewer inputs, the higher the likelihood of success. To paraphrase Richard Dennis, the mentor and financial backer of the famed Turtle Traders, when he was asked how he was able to make so much more money than anyone else in the room: "There is a lot less here than meets the eye."

There is much to be said for both trend and countertrend trading methods and tactics. In the trading environment of summer 2009, with the major industrialized countries having already cut their interest rates significantly, it is likely that because of the decrease of the previous interest rate differentials that created and fed the former carry trade we would be finding ourselves more often in smaller trading ranges marked by more sideways price behavior, that is, more countertrending markets.

TRADING PHILOSOPHY

CHAPTER 10

TRADING PSYCHOLOGY

Hardwired to Trade

You will find that as you learn how to trade, it is not enough to be told something, read about it, and then experience it in the market. Taken cumulatively as an approach to learning, that still amounts to a series of brief impressions. To have a method or a trading plan truly hardwired into your head takes many, many impressions or, ideally, many months or even years of demo or live trading. Gaining that experience takes discipline. It's not enough to say that you believe in a method or in yourself; you have to know it subconsciously, and that takes repetition, which takes time. Regardless of how much you read or are told about the way a trading method or indicator works, in our experience you probably will make mistakes in execution. This happens for many reasons, most of which have very little to do with the market and much to do with your internal beliefs and experience. The saying "the map is not the territory" makes sense from a trading perspective. By this we mean that you can study the map beforehand all you want, but once you are sitting by the screen alone in your trading room considering markets and potential trade setups, it is a completely different experience, making your behavior less predictable.

We once had an acquaintance say to us that he knew he needed to understand the method but that he was looking forward to acquiring the "intuition" of a successful trader as soon as he could. We caution against this type of approach because student traders should not even consider the idea that intuition can play a part in trading until they have the mechanics of a method down cold, meaning hundreds if not thousands of demo and live trades logged. Intuition does not come from thinking or studying; it comes from experience, which costs time. You have to learn to crawl before you can walk, and in trading that means that hope quickly gives way to frustration and fear; if you can get past that, you may find yourself standing at the crossroads of quitting and eventual success. It is from there that your journey will begin. We know it is hard for clients to hear this because it is not what they want to hear. People have a habit of not remembering and recording things they do not want to hear.

This book attempts to help you become a better trader but will leave only a shallow impression unless you draw up your own trading plan and demo trade over and over. We will discuss ways to draw up a trading plan in Chapter 13.

Patience

Patience is equal in value to discipline in this game; both are priceless. We've always suspected that the reason 90 to 95 percent of retail traders lose their money is that they have no patience.

There once was a great bond trader named Charlie D. who made quite a name for himself in the business. He was a pit trader in Chicago, and government bond traders in Tokyo would lament that trading in bonds was never the same after Charlie D. passed on. That may have seemed to be true, but it probably had more to do with global economics than with one man moving on, though you never know.

Other traders liked to tell the story of Charlie's first month or two in the pit. On his first day he got into the pit, elbowed his way to a spot, and stood there all day and watched. The other traders loved to see a new face because they usually could skin him of his holdings fairly quickly. The bond pit in the 1980s and 1990s was easily the biggest game in town and was a mean, roiling mass of men as brutal as any where big money was involved. They would scream at Charlie, and he would not trade, just watch. They would jab pencils at him menacingly, questioning his manhood, but he still would not trade with them, just watch. They despised him for taking up a spot in the crowded pit, and in the middle of their trading they constantly tried to shove him off and push him down, but he would not yield. The regular bond traders were as persistent and stubborn as Charlie and refused to let up on him. He still wouldn't trade, though, just watch, day after day and week after week.

To make a long story short, Charlie D. learned the game and went on to be one of the biggest traders in the biggest pit. He did it because he was patient and would not be compromised even in extreme conditions. His baptism in the pit may sound childish, but to survive 10 minutes in such a hostile environment, let alone a day, then a week, and then a month, while holding his ground and not trading with the pack was amazing.

We need to understand the importance of taking the time to learn before risking hard-earned money, and that requires patience. The rest—reading charts, coordinating time frames, identifying significant support and resistance and formations, and understanding the necessary overlays and indicators—is simple compared with holding one's fire until the time is right.

Discipline

We hear the word *discipline* a lot when people talk about trading philosophies and trading psychology. Most of us heard the word a lot in our formative years too. The concept is the same. Discipline when you were younger might have meant getting up early to do your morning paper route, making sure to do your chores before breakfast, or being on time for school. Many people learned a higher level of discipline in the military or when they had children of their own to worry about and supervise. For some people discipline may mean limiting oneself to a couple of beers at the ball game or to two martinis while out with the girls.

Discipline in trading is very similar. It means not throwing good money after bad and not succumbing to the rush of making fast money. This is particularly important after a trader has had a profitable streak. You will find that once you've had a profitable trade or a string of profitable trades, you miss not being in the market. You also may start to think that because you have this cushion of profit, it's easier to take risks. When you recognize this behavior, it should set off alarm bells. Disciplined traders wait patiently for their setups and treat the risk the same way regardless of the outcome of their last trade or their last 10 trades. The same traits people exhibit in their professional and social lives will show up in their trading habits.

The good thing about discipline, as any drill sergeant will tell you, is that it can be taught. Often the hardest things for people to do are to have the discipline to evaluate themselves honestly and identify their weaknesses. If they can come to terms with that and come up with a plan to discipline themselves, they are on their way to becoming successful in more than just trading. To simplify things, remember that the only goal a trader should have is to have the discipline to follow her trading plan, which we will be covering shortly.

Discipline also means always using a stop-loss order, which is an order that is entered after you initiate a position that automatically will take you out of that position with a loss if the market moves against you. We will cover Stop-loss orders in more detail in Chapter 12. It is impossible for us to talk to you about trading without making sure you know how to use stop-loss orders.

Psychology

There are many misconceptions about the type of people successful traders are. For example, are they are creative mavericks with aggressive personalities? This is not altogether untrue but is the opposite of the case in our estimation. It was said of one very successful trader we know that he seemed to worry more about what he wanted on his pizza than about his position in the market. His approach to life and his approach to trading could be described as very laid back.

Successful traders tend to be good listeners who are thoughtful, very patient, humble, and even sensitive. Although we might not describe our head trader at Trading-U.com, Al Gaskill, as laid back, we can say he is very thoughtful and one of the most patient individuals we know. Bill Williams, who is a successful trader and also has a doctorate in psychology, looks for the quality he calls "reality-oriented" to see whether people can become successful traders.

Being reality-oriented means having the ability to *listen*. In our estimation, it also means being someone who understands that life is about sharing the stage and being aware of not just one's own surroundings but the needs of others in those surroundings. Individuals like that, who know and admit they have weaknesses and understand the emotions brought on by attachment, are able to learn from their mistakes and take direction much more easily than are people who want the spotlight and see themselves as being smarter and more deserving than others on that stage. Being competitive helps, but in a way that says that the individual wants to help herself for the right reasons. Reality-oriented refers to someone accustomed to going with the flow, not trying to orchestrate the flow. It also entails understanding that there are at least two sides to every story and knowing the value and freedom of not being judgmental. Being laid back is much better than being aggressive or emotional. It is far easier to absorb something while relaxed than it is while tense. Equally, it is far easier to grasp the reality of a situation when you have no attachment to the outcome. It is that axiom which makes demo trading so important. It is far easier to learn in a simulated, less fearful environment where mistakes are learning experiences rather than financial losses. Save the overthinking for important subjects such as what you want on your pizza.

One of the biggest personality warning signs for traders comes from people who are accustomed to getting other people to change their minds or willing people to do things that aren't in their best interests. Salespeople come to mind. If you are used to being able to manipulate people, you will be in for a surprise when you trade, because you cannot cajole or bluff the market. It is said that the worst products have the best marketers, and nowhere is this truer than in the brokerage industry. Because of this, brokers tend to have very limited success as traders. Brokers are not alone on that list, however. Lawyers also often struggle as traders. Many advanced education professionals, coming from a field in which linear logic, not intuition, is practiced, have an uphill struggle too.

The same personality traits that give people problems in life will give them problems in trading; only in trading those traits will be magnified. Your personality will play an important part in whether you are successful in trading. We do not, however, want to ignore the importance of your trading method. The thing that is going to make you or break you as a trader is the method you follow. There probably has been more written on trader psychology than on actual trading methods over the last five years. This is most likely the case because successful trading methodologies are relatively simple when taught in the right order. The subject of how people have a penchant for complicating nearly everything they touch is not.

✓ We are seeing more and more writers and trading educators covering the subject of trading psychology. Those who stand out for us are Bill Williams and his daughter, Justine Williams-Lara. Chapters 3, 4, and 5 of the second edition of their book *Trading Chaos* are very insightful in their analysis of human behavior. Van Tharp's books and workshops are well regarded by top-level traders, as is Mark Douglas's book *Trading in the Zone*.

The thing to remember is that trading is about making money, yet somehow, particularly for beginners, that gets lost in the emotions and egos. The way to stay focused on making money is to study your course material, then back test to the point where you recognize signals instantly regardless of background noise, and then demo trade until you are profitable. Next trade micro lots, again until you are profitable, and then trade mini contracts until you are satisfied with your risk-reward ratio and winning percentage.

Get used to the fact that you are going to be wrong and are going to have days when you lose money. Any business has expenses, and trading is no different. Always remember that trading is not about being right or wrong or even about thinking; it is about executing one's plan.

CHAPTER 11

TRADING THE APPROPRIATE TIME FRAME

If you decide to trade, the first thing you need to determine is the time frame in which you are going to trade. It is important that the time frame fit your lifestyle. There are three general categories of trading styles. The first is position, or end-of-day, trend trading, which tends to have the most favorable risk-reward ratio and also takes up the smallest amount of time per day. The second is swing trading, for which you don't need to be sitting in front of a computer screen; however, signals can come at any time of the day, and so you need to be able to enter orders from a portable electronic device. The third is day trading, which takes a high degree of concentration and requires the trader to be sitting in front of the computer; this type of trader has a higher winning percentage but a less favorable risk-reward ratio.

Position, or End-of-Day, Trading

Position, or end-of-day, trading is fairly straightforward in that the trader is taking trade signals on the basis of price behavior on the daily charts. Once you've completed your trading plan and know what qualifies as a trade signal, the only time you will enter orders is just before the end of the trading day at 5 p.m. EST. As an end-of-day trader you leave yourself enough time to analyze the markets you trade and enter your orders just before the close. (Though the market trades around the clock from Sunday 5 p.m. EST through Friday 5 p.m. EST, it is common parlance to refer to 5 p.m. EST as the close because it marks the change from one day to the next on the daily chart.) While doing your analysis, you determine whether the trade is a trend or a countertrend on the basis of the stance of your daily chart and look to the weekly and monthly charts for confirmation.

Once you are in a trade, you base your stop-loss order on the combination of a percentage of your account and price structure (support or resistance). You do not have to check back in until just before 5 p.m. EST the next day. Because you don't make a trading decision while the candle is still open and have a stop-loss order in place, you have to make a decision only once a day. Because position traders trade a longer-term time frame, they generally do not consider fundamental news releases when they make entering and exiting decisions. They always, however, have stop-loss orders in place as a precaution against unforeseen events that could change the higher time frame trends. A word of caution on stops: Even with a stop in place, there is always the possibility that markets will jump wildly higher or lower and the possibility that a market will gap through one's stop, and so it is always a good idea to check in once a day to see the status of one's account.

Let us discuss some examples of trade signals given on the daily chart in GBPUSD that are based on a simple method involving trendlines and stochastics in the summer of 2008. The signals come on the closes of the candles marked by the horizontal lines and are based on a trendline break and a corresponding signal by the stochastic when it either crosses down through its overbought line or crosses up through its oversold line on a closing basis. To exit, or cover the trade, we would use the same trendline penetration but would need only a cross of the stochastic's red and blue lines on a closing basis. To reverse our position, however, we would be using the cross down through the upper (overbought) stochastic level or the cross up through the lower (oversold) stochastic level.

One of the drawbacks of end-of-day trading is that when you get into sideways or countertrending markets such as the one that occurred at the beginning of July 2008 (see Figure 11-1), you probably are going to take losses more frequently. We see a sell signal in the beginning of the month followed by a signal to exit that trade one week later at a loss. Regardless of the losses, you must continue to take the next trigger. The payback for continuing to take the next trigger is shown by the sell signal in mid-July that preceded the sharp sell-off that occurred in August 2008. A move such as this will make up for more than a few smaller losses.

In position trading you cannot be bothered by losses or drawdowns. You cannot be scared to take the next trigger, and

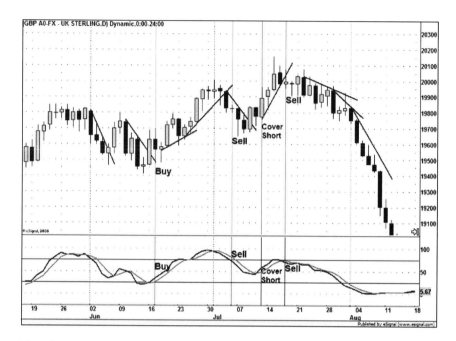

Figure 11-1 End-of-Day Trade Signals

you have to be able to let a profit run. One of the hardest things to do in trading is to allow a profit to run, particularly after a trader has had several losers in a row. Many traders have exited a winning trade too soon or even failed to take the trade that led to the big winner, particularly after sustaining several losses in a row. Being a position trader often means going through periods in which you have more losers than winners; this highlights how important it is to get those long-running winners. When you do get a winner and learn to let the trades run, you will find that on average your winners are much larger than your losers; this accounts for the favorable risk-reward ratio that position traders enjoy compared with traders who work the lower time frames.

If you are in a position trade and find yourself constantly checking the price to see where your position is, you probably have too much at risk on the trade. In other words, you have too large a position on; this also is known as overtrading. If you find you are getting up in the middle of the night to check your position, you definitely have too much at risk. In a position trade—or any trade—you should be risking only a <u>small percentage</u> of your overall risk capital. For professionals this may be as little as 0.5 to 1 percent. For beginners, who are often undercapitalized by definition, it should never be over 5 percent and preferably should be closer to 2 percent.

The biggest advantage of position trading is that you do not have to spend eight or more hours in front of a computer screen and have to check in only once a day. The fact that you are trading on the higher time frames also means that you will catch larger price movements. The disadvantage of position trading is the other side of the risk-reward coin: Your losses will tend to be larger than they would be if you were trading a smaller time frame. We recommend always starting out with just one contract per position trade and keeping your stop far enough away from price so that you will not be knocked out prematurely by the larger intraday price swings in markets that are due to fundamental news releases and other day-to-day happenings in the world and in financial markets. Your stop generally should be placed just beyond the last swing high or low on the chart. If you are not comfortable with the idea of losing that much money—the distance from where you entered the trade to where your stop is—you should not take the trade.

We often hear from beginners that it is not realistic to keep the risk per trade at such low levels. We disagree wholeheartedly. With the advent of micro contracts—$1,000 face value and a margin rate of just $20 per contract at 50 to 1—there should be no problem staying within reasonable risk parameters.

Swing Trading

Swing trading involves shorter time frames than the daily charts; this generally means trading from the 240-, 60-, and 15-minute charts. The time you could be in a swing trade can range from hours to days, and the trade can be a trend trade or a countertrend trade. Often swing trades are countertrend trades as they take advantage of the secondary moves that often follow extended impulsive (trend) moves. The term *swing trade* comes from the trader's action of swinging long or short. Swing traders in general are less concerned with long-term trends than with waiting for setups or patterns on the chart that they recognize. Some swing traders are in the market all the time as they take every buy and sell signal in their trading plan. They know that although they will have losers (drawdowns), by being properly capitalized and using sound money management, they will be in a position to catch the biggest moves. Swing traders, like all technical traders, always should have stops placed that are based on a percentage of the account size or risk capital and structure on the chart. Like position traders, swing traders need to keep their stops far enough away from price to avoid being knocked out of positions prematurely by day-to-day volatility and must be willing to hold their trades through scheduled fundamental news releases.

There are probably nearly as many swing trading strategies employed in the markets as there are traders who use them successfully. The one thing they all have in common is that they trade higher time frames than day traders do, and it matters little to them whether they are long or short or are going with or against the long-term trend. Because they have to check their positions only periodically, they don't have to be on the screen when they are in the market, though they do need to be able to monitor their positions and look at charts occasionally to gauge their strategies. These are the traders who can make trading decisions on the basis of a look at a chart on a portable device or cell phone or have the computer send their cell phones an alert or text message when the price gets to a certain level or a technical indicator gives a signal they rely on. They also rely on trailing stops and OCO (order cancels order) orders and other automated features on current trading platforms.

Figure 11-2 shows examples of two swing trades; they are identified by the gray vertical lines, which were determined by coordinating the 60-minute chart on top with the 240-minute chart below and using the MACD zero line cross, intermediate-term trendlines, and the weekly central pivot point for entries. The trader determined that he would take buy signals generated by trendline penetrations and zero line crosses on the MACD on a closing basis on the 60-minute chart if that occurred above the weekly pivot point and the MACD was above the zero line on a closing basis on the 240-minute chart. Once the trade was initiated, a stop-loss was entered at a price equal to 2 percent of his account balance or just below the low of the previous candle he entered on, depending on which number gave the trade more room. He would use the MACD

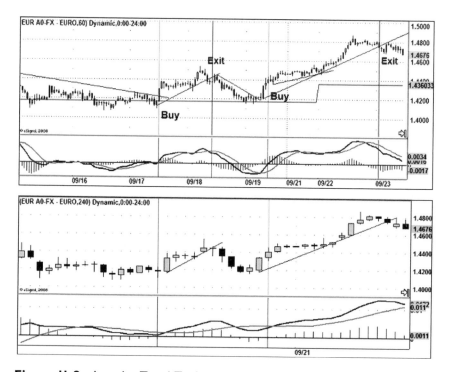

Figure 11-2 Intraday Trend Trading Using 240-Minute and 60-Minute Charts

and trendlines on the 240-minute chart to monitor and manage the trade and a combination of a trendline break and an MACD cross of its trigger line on the 60-minute chart to exit.

Short-Term, or Day, Trading

Short-term, or day, trading means that the trader generally does not hold positions overnight and trades a lower time frame chart such as a 15-minute or a 5-minute chart or a chart with an even lower time frame. Day trading is popular for several reasons, especially its simplicity once the skill has been mastered. It is a business with very low start-up costs and a technically unlimited upside. Although there is the possibility that individuals can lose more than they fund an account with, brokerage houses have gotten much better at closing an account holder's trades out for her rather than let her incur a debit balance, that is, let the account drop to less than zero, leaving a debt. There definitely is a dark side to trading, and to day trading in particular, as the exhilaration of the potential for fast money attracts addictive personalities the way gambling casinos do. For many beginners day trading is the way they were introduced to trading, and brokers and dealers rely on a steady flow of new account holders coming through their doors. Many forex brokers, unlike stock or commodities brokers, will accept credit cards to keep their clients trading.

Day traders generally trade more contracts than do position or swing traders because they trade smaller time frames and generally remain on the screen while in a position. The larger trade size means they can take smaller bites out of the market and make just as much as the higher time frame traders make, only over a shorter period.

The same techniques for distinguishing between trend and countertrend setups and the use of stop placement that is based on percentage of the account and chart structure apply to day trading too. Day trading is very much a microcosm of position trading and swing trading. The only difference is that in day trading one must be aware of scheduled economic releases and other world or financial market developments that can affect price movement over the short term or intermediate term.

In day trading, you always should exit your position 5 to 10 minutes ahead of major scheduled economic releases. We use www.forexfactory.com for its calendar and anything marked in red or orange to be a major release. After an important news release we do not enter trades until the candles on the charts with the shortest time frame stop showing dojis and start showing wider candle bodies. Remember that dojis show indecision and the wider bodies show that trade is being facilitated.

For day trading we recommend using the 15-minute chart for timing and patterns, the 60-minute chart for direction and confirmation, and 5-minute or 3-minute charts to help time entries and exits.

Figure 11-3 shows an example of a day trade in which the trader sees an existing sell signal in place on the 60-minute chart and waits for a favorable setup on the 15-minute chart, which comes at 9:15 a.m. CST and gives him a nice day trade.

Taking a more detailed look at this example, we see that the 60-minute chart on the bottom gave a sell signal at the top of a sideways channel on the basis of a trendline violation and a stochastic overbought cross, accompanied by divergence in the MACD. As day traders, we also would have checked the calendar at www.forexfactory.com or one of the other complimentary services and known we had a significant news release out in the form of the U.S. durable goods figures at 7:30 a.m. A durable goods report is a compilation of the orders received by U.S. manufacturers for big-ticket items such as cars, household appliances, and computers; it is released by the U.S. Census Bureau.

As day traders we would wait till after the durable goods release before determining whether this market was worth

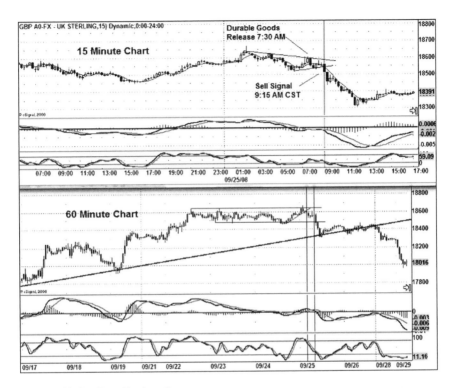

Figure 11-3 Day Trading Setup

the risk of trading. As it turned out, this market gave us a short-term resistance line created by the early a.m. highs and the knee-jerk rally on the core durable goods number, which came in weaker than expected at −3.0 as opposed to the expected −0.5.

Before the news release in Figure 11-3 we had a sell signal on the 60-minute chart hours earlier, and on the 15-minute chart we see that the MACD had dropped below the zero line and stayed below zero despite the short-lived rally that followed the 7:30 a.m. CST release. We know that this is bearish behavior, and it also tells us that the trend on the next lower time frames is going to be lower also. After slumping lower, the market tried to rally one more time and ended up forming a small symmetrical triangle on the 15-minute chart. Symmetrical triangles, as we know from Chapter 6, tend to be continuation patterns that are likely to break out in the same direction in which they were moving when they formed their base. In this case, the base was created while moving north to south, or higher to lower, and the market was exhibiting a pattern of lower highs. However, we still would wait for a close outside the triangle before initiating a trade. Once we did get that signal as marked on the chart, GBPUSD fell over 200 pips in the next three hours, which would have led to a profit of over 600 pips if we had sold three contracts short. On our 15-minute chart we also have a 5-simple moving average set to the close that we would use to keep us in the trade. As long as candles closed below the 5-SMA line, which is marked in black, we would continue to hold our short position. As you can see, when we are day trading, we need to pull a lot of observations, indicators, and tools together. We also need to be able to make decisions quickly and with confidence.

Successful day traders are definitely rarer than market students care to know and admit, yet there are few jobs or businesses that are better to have.

If you decide to learn to trade for yourself, you will have to decide which trading time frame best suits your lifestyle.

PART 5

RISK MANAGEMENT

CHAPTER 12

RISK AND MONEY MANAGEMENT

Stop-Loss Orders and Margin

We need to cover volatility before we talk about risk management. Volatility is the rate of the change in price over a specific period. The faster price rises or falls through time, the higher the volatility is. Volatility is calculated as the standard deviation of the percentage change in the daily price. Simply put, the faster a market moves in one direction, the more volatile it becomes and the more likely we are to see above-average price movement relative to previous price behavior. Another way to say this is that the higher the volatility in a market is, the more money a trader will have to risk per trade.

One way traders can limit their risk is by using stop-loss orders. What's important for traders and investors to know about stop-loss orders is that although they work most of the time, there is no guarantee they will be filled at your price or, in forex markets, filled at all. There are times when markets can gap higher or lower, particularly on the Sunday opening, leaving a stop order filled at a different price or not filled at all. Because of this possibility, it is best to monitor your account at all times when you are in the market.

In our trading accounts we always look to risk no more than 2 percent per trade or 6 percent per day of our risk capital. If we are sizing up a setup or trade and determine that the risk is outside our parameters, we do not take the trade. Before we cover risk, though, we need to understand the dangers of margin. In commodity futures you often can control 100 percent of a commodity by putting down 3 to 7 percent of the cost of the physical commodity. An example is gold. In a commodity account you can buy 33 ounces of gold or one mini gold contract, worth approximately $29,700, for $1,100 down. The margin for gold thus is 27 to 1: $1,100(27) = $29,700. The danger in this is that if you bought a mini gold contract in a $5,000 account and gold moved lower by $35 per ounce—as it did on August 11, 2008—and you did not have a stop order placed, you would have lost over $1,100, or 22 percent of your account, in one day. Margin is always a dangerous proposition for untried traders, but when combined with volatility it is treacherous.

In futures we have mini contracts, yet with the surge in volatility in commodity prices over the last several years, many smaller account holders have been priced out of the market as they have been forced to risk higher percentages of their account balances. In forex the margins are even higher, and that makes it more treacherous for novice traders. Margin in forex can range from 50 to 1 all the way up to 400 to 1. However, aside from the standard contract, which has a $100,000 face value and can be controlled with $2,000 down at 50 to 1 or with

$1,000 at 100 to 1, there is also a $10,000 contract that can be controlled for $100 at 100 to 1 and a $1,000 contract that can be controlled with $10 down at 100 to 1. Because of these smaller contract sizes, it is easier to stay within the 2 percent stop-loss rule whether you are trading a $10,000 account or a $1,000 account. It is important to remember, however, that whatever the margin rate is, if you are wrong on a trade, you will lose the full percentage value loss of that instrument; that means that if you go long a standard 100,000 EURUSD contract and the euro drops 2 percent that day against the U.S. currency, you will have lost $2,000.

When we are short-term trading, or day trading, we generally don't plan on leaving the screen while we are in a trade. We try to go with multiple contracts that give us the freedom to take a portion of our position off at a profit that is based on market structure and short-term behavior, letting us to allow the balance to run on the basis of longer-term market behavior. If we are trading longer-term time-frames, or end-of-day—using a daily chart—we will trade at least one contract. Before taking a trade, we figure out what 2 percent of our risk capital is (0.02 multiplied by the net liquid value of combined futures and forex accounts), and this is the amount we can risk per trade. Along with giving you your stop-loss, or the amount risked on the trade, this amount will help determine your lot size.

For example, let's say your risk capital accounts are $10,000, and so you may risk 0.02(10,000) = $200. We may know from experience that our risk per trade on the British pound is approximately 30 pips per contract, or $30 per mini contract. Thus, if we can risk $200 on a day trade in GBPUSD, we divide $30 into $200 and get 6.66. We round down to 6, which means we can trade six minis, or a $60,000 block of GBPUSD, and we must put a 30-pip stop on that trade once it has been entered. Therefore, if we sell six minis at 198.00 on a day trade, we need to place a buy stop at 198.30. If that distance seems too short and thus unreasonable in light of the volatility in the market and the structure on the chart, we pass on the trade or put on fewer contracts. If we choose to take a position trade for a longer-term period, we can sell two at 198.00 and place a 90-pip stop or a buy stop at 198.90 to keep the possible loss at 2 percent; similarly, we can sell one short GBPUSD at 198.00 and place a buy stop up at 199.80, or 180 pips above the short position, to maintain a 2 percent loss.

Getting back to the six-lot day trade, by risking just 2 percent in GBPUSD, we would be able to take at least two more trades in other pairs. Alternatively, we could choose to risk 1 percent, or $100, that is, three mini contracts, or a $30,000 block in GBPUSD and have the freedom to trade up to five more pairs, keeping the total risk per day to approximately 6 percent of the risk capital. This way we have room to day trade several positions or position trade several pairs and keep our total exposure to 6 percent. If there is an adverse move against our positions, we adjust our stops and risk accordingly, always maintaining a total exposure of just 6 percent on all open positions. If our account draws down, so does our exposure on future trades. As the account grows, we're able to increase our trading size. By placing the physical stop we learn discipline and also are assured of maintaining a reasonable risk-reward ratio by professional standards if something unforeseen happens in our lives or in the marketplace. Always remember to check to see if you have any active working stop orders when you exit your trading platform.

Exiting Positions

When it comes to exiting positions or trades, we recommend the equal but opposite approach. That means that once we are in a position, we are looking for price and indicator behavior similar to that which prompted us to take the signal initially. If a trader is tying together candle (price) behavior against existing support or resistance and short-term trendline penetration on a closing basis and is using the order of operation of the technical indicators to enter trades, then he will look for similar price action in the opposite direction to exit trades. If we took a buy signal because a short-term bear trendline was penetrated and the stochastic was confirmed, we would look to exit as the market went up and tested its intermediate-term trendline, giving us indications that it was turning lower. Similarly, if we enter a trade and it does not go our way but starts to roll back against us, the market will give us the same indications it just gave us to get in, but this time we will heed them by exiting. By following the same strategies to enter and exit trades, a trader is more likely to exit most trades before her stop order is executed. Depending on the time frames the trader is following, he will have the option of taking indications and signals on lower time frames in the face of support or resistance to help protect a profit on the entire position or a portion of the position.

Figure 12-1 shows an example of a market in a downtrend, which is marked by the black trend line above the price. Our signal to take a trade is a change-of-direction candle that closes beyond the moving average and is accompanied by a bearish cross of the stochastic trigger line. The benefit to the trader of

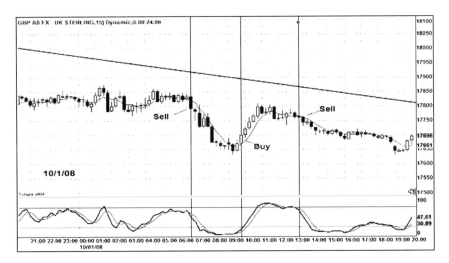

Figure 12-1 Entry Followed by Equal but Opposite Exit

using a simple tactic like this is that if the market accelerates, the trader stays in the trade, but if the trade rolls over and corrects, the trader exits. A stop-loss would be placed just beyond the last swing high or low once the trade was entered.

By following the equal but opposite principle in exiting a trade, we also are practicing another important trading concept: "Always see both sides of the market." Like "lose your opinion, not your money," this is a reminder that it is the market that determines when you exit or enter a trade, not you. Once a trader exits a position, it is very important to remember to go back and cancel any working stop or limit orders that may have been left on the trading platform.

Figure 12-2 provides a more detailed example of using the same signals to enter trades that one uses to exit them and/or reverse, which means taking a position in the opposite direction to the one you just exited. For this example the signal will be a change-of-direction candle accompanied by a stochastic cross above the oversold line for buys and below the overbought line for sells. We always place our stop-loss order just beyond the last swing high or low, and when we get a signal in the opposite direction of our trade, we will reverse. We will not, however, reverse our position if we are stopped out. We've marked the signals along with the places where we've placed our stop-loss orders.

In the first trade, which is labeled #1 Buy, we've placed our sell stop order below the last swing low. The trade went our way nicely, and we exited and reversed on the same change-of-direction candle marked #2 Sell. At this point we would cancel our original stop-loss order and place our new stop above

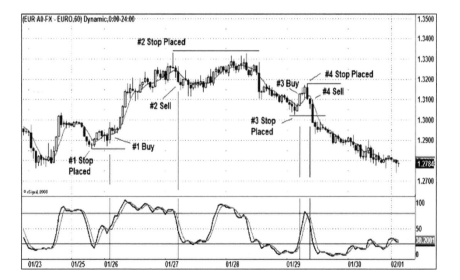

Figure 12-2   Entry Followed by Stop-Loss Entry Followed by Exit

the last swing high. Despite the fact that the market and the stochastic went against our position, we never got a change-of-direction candle until the stochastic already had turned down, and the market remained below our stop. For #3 Buy we exited the short and entered a long position and placed our sell stop below the last swing low, remembering to cancel our previous buy stop. After a bearish change-of-direction candle shortly afterward, we took a loss on the long trade and reversed our position by going short at #4 Sell and then placed a new buy stop above the last swing high, remembering to cancel our previous sell stop.

Note in Figure 12-2 that we never got stopped out of a position. Though we came close on #2 Sell, we stuck to our plan and avoided a loss. The only time we responded was when the market gave us a signal. This is the way it should be. You should always be in the right frame of mind to react appropriately to what the market does but not to anything else. The connection between exiting the current position and canceling the previous stop, plus entering a new stop if necessary, is also important. You will find that in demo trading you will get in the habit of always checking with yourself and checking your trading platform to make sure that you've canceled your previous stop and, if you are currently in a position, that you have a stop just beyond the last swing high or low. You also may trail a stop behind your position, that is, move your stop along with the market when you are showing a profit, though we recommend that you be careful when moving a stop and just leave the stop where you placed it. Perhaps you can use a breakeven stop if you are showing a healthy profit, but it is best to monitor the market closely for your signal and not concern yourself with the prospects of winning and losing. Moving the stop too close to the market price can cause you to be taken out of a position prematurely and also shows nervousness on your part. If you know your method well and have back tested and demo traded it thoroughly, there is no need to be nervous. Waiting and taking signals and stop placement orders should be business as usual for you after several hundred demo trades. You will find that the less thinking you do, the better it is for your account balance.

Always Have the Appropriate Phone Numbers on Hand

You need to have significant information within easy reach at all times. Significant information includes your account numbers and pass codes to all accounts, along with the phone numbers of your points of contact at the firms where your accounts are held and the direct numbers to the trade desk or dealing desk that has access to your accounts. The Internet is reliable, seemingly more so every day, but there is always a chance that something will go wrong somewhere and that it could happen at a very inappropriate—that is, risky—time for you.

You need to know ahead of time that if your Internet connection or landline goes down, you can pick up a cell phone and call your dealer to confirm your position and make sure your stop is placed. When that tricky time in which you lose connectivity with your account and money does come, you will be able to remain much calmer if you have all the numbers you need within reach.

CHAPTER 13

CREATING A TRADING PLAN AND KEEPING A TRADING JOURNAL

B efore you begin to trade in a demo account, it is imperative that you write out your trading plan. Don't start with bad habits by trying to wing it; you will only frustrate yourself and eventually blow out your account. This is very important because when you write it out yourself and then adjust and fine-tune it, you are going to find that when you are on the screen, you will be much more tuned in to what the market is telling you to do. Unless you write out your plan yourself, rewrite it, and adjust it over the course of your demo trading, you will not hardwire yourself properly. The learning process is essentially threefold:

1. Read and/or see information and/or instructions—such as this book.
2. See the information used in an example.
3. Execute the plan by yourself, using the information and instructions in a simulated environment.

Once we get to step 3, we are adding experience to the learning process. Worthwhile experiences will encourage us to continue to pursue this process. Those experiences will come from doing what we are supposed to do when we are supposed to do it. Remembering what you are supposed to do and when you are supposed to do it becomes much more likely if you have read it and then written it down yourself as opposed to just reading it. You also need to contribute to the process of creating your trading plan, not just copying one of ours. You will understand your plan much better if you construct it yourself. This book will help you because you can go back and research the tools and setups and signals you will need to understand to create and execute your plan. At Trading-U.com we teach that the most important step in the learning process is completing a sound trading plan. We will help you do this by showing you an example of a trading plan later in this chapter.

A trading plan is a definitive document that spells out everything you will do as a trader. It specifies the time frame charts you will use, the indicators and overlays you will use on those charts, and how you will use those tools to determine your entries and exits. It determines how much money you are willing to risk per trade and per day. More important, it is a road map you can consult at any time before entering a trade, during the management of a trade, and after a trade.

The importance of a trading plan cannot be overstated. Although the human brain can, in the blink of an eye, take in far more information than a person could ever use, it can focus on only six or seven things at once. Because of this you can see how important it is that you be taught the correct information and learn it thoroughly enough that when the time comes, you will be able to absorb most of the initial steps of analyzing a particular market, such as support and resistance and trendlines, chart and candle formations, and technical indicators, at a glance, allowing you to focus on the most important steps in the trading process: the handful of developments that determine your actual trade signals and the price behavior that determines your stop-loss strategy and profit determinants. Analyzing and then trading can be viewed as a pyramid in which 90 to 95 percent of the process is the foundation, after which comes the base and then the building blocks; trading is the tip where you are going to make a living from a handful of actual trading decisions. The fact is that you have spelled out 90 to 95 percent of the core knowledge needs in your trading plan. You will find that it will be much easier to remain patient yet focused if you have a time-tested trading plan within easy reach.

You also will find that trading can be stressful because as humans we are programmed from the beginning to improve our situation and surroundings and have emotions. This means we have an innate urge toward progress, and when that drive is slowed or stopped, we become frustrated. Frustration creates stress. If we feel that our progress has been stopped or even reversed, as happens when a trader is experiencing a position going against him or her, that frustration can turn to anger and fear. We will always have emotions; the difference between a professional trader and a beginner is that the professional is prepared for the emotions and the stress they create. This preparation starts with writing out a trading plan. Regardless of the emotional desire to close out the position at a loss and stop the fear or try to fight the market by increasing the position, professional traders follow their trading plans automatically because that is how they have programmed themselves and because they know it is their only defense.

Here is an example of a trading plan that uses some of the tools we have taught you in this book.

Sample Trading Plan

Our sample trading plan has the following elements:

Method: Trading in the same direction as the higher time frame trend.

Calendar: For trading intraday, always check the news calendar at forexfactory.com or FXstreet.com for the daily schedule of news releases. Always exit existing short-term positions 5 to 10 minutes ahead of those scheduled news releases.

Charts: Daily and weekly candlestick charts to select market and direction; 15-minute and 60-minute candlestick charts for the setup and signal.

Overlays: Horizontal support and resistance levels, trendlines, and appropriate pivot points.

Indicators: Stochastic (14, 3, 3) and MACD (26–12–9).

Setup: Identify and record short-term trends on weekly and daily charts for the markets covered on the basis of the position of current trendlines and the stochastic. Find markets in which the short-term trends on the daily and weekly charts are pointing in the same direction. Markets you need to be cautious about are those in which the trends on the weekly and daily charts are moving in the same direction but price is at or near historical lows or highs (support or resistance) and in which there is double divergence or more on the daily chart as measured by the MACD. Once you've selected the markets that fit these criteria, look for setups and trade signals on the 15-minute chart at or near support or resistance that are going in the same direction as the charts with higher time frames. Once you identify possible trade signals, filter or confirm those signals with the 60-minute chart. If the trend on the 60-minute chart already is pointing in the same direction as the potential signal on the 15-minute chart, take the trade. If the short-term trend on the 60-minute chart is not moving in the same direction as the potential signal on the 15-minute chart but there is an indication of indecision such as a shooting star or a hammer and then a price close beyond that candle that is indicative of a possible reversal and a shift in momentum such as a stochastic trigger line cross, take the trade. If the short-term trend on the 60-minute chart conflicts with the potential signal on the 15-minute chart, meaning there is no indication of indecision or a shift in momentum on the higher time frame, do not take the trade. We also are cautious about entering trades with multiple divergence shown by the MACD on the intraday charts that are opposite to our position.

Signals: Trendline violation with stochastic confirmation on a closing basis and/or a close beyond the high or low of an appropriate doji (hammer for buy, shooting star for sell) on support or resistance. The candle to close below the high or low of the doji or inside candle is most often by definition a change-of-direction candle.

Exit and Stop: Always place stop just beyond the last swing high or swing low in the direction opposite to the position you took. For a buy, or long, position, place a sell stop below the last swing low, keeping within your risk parameter: 1 to 3 percent of the account per trade. For a sell, or short, position, place a buy stop above the last swing high, again making sure to keep your risk at an acceptable level. You also can use a 2-ATR stop as long as the risk on the trade is acceptable to you. Once you are in the trade, be mindful that you must start to draw a new trendline that will provide support or resistance for the trend you just entered. Our entry signal is the same condition that marks a shift in the short-term trend. A price close on a closing basis beyond this new trendline, moving against our position, also will serve as our signal to exit the trade. If the trade goes in our direction by the same distance as the money we've risked, we can move our stop to breakeven. For taking a profit we key off existing trendlines and pivot points. If you entered the position on a short-term trendline violation, you should monitor price behavior as it approaches and tests the intermediate-term trendline or the next daily pivot point. If it looks to be pausing—showing indecisive candles—on an area of support or resistance, take the profit; if you are trading multiple contracts, take a portion of the profit. If it closes beyond the intermediate-term trendline, look for it to trade to the long-term trendline. You can deploy the same strategy by using pivot points. If the market moves beyond a pivot level, look for it to move on to the next pivot level. If the market moves beyond all existing support or resistance on the chart, continue to update the trendline created by the current move and look for the order of operation of the technical indicators to give you an exit signal. To exit a trade, look for the same or a similar price action that prompted you to enter the trade. If you are in a trade and it does not go in the direction of the signal, you do not need to wait for your stop to get hit. You can exit the trade on the basis of a combination of a short-term trendline penetration on a closing basis and a cross of the MACD and its trigger line on a closing basis. A change-of-direction candle, which often creates trendline penetrations, also can be used to exit a trade. Keep in mind that the longer you are in a trade that is not going in the direction of the original signal, the more your risk will increase. You can always come out of a trade and go back in if you get another signal.

The charts that follow demonstrate two trades that this trading plan would qualify.

The weekly chart in the lower panel of Figure 13-1 highlights the week ending January 9, 2009; this pattern turns out to have been a change-of-direction candle after a shooting star. We also have the stochastic crossing down, and we have drawn a new bear trendline extending into the future after the reversal of the December uptrend. All these developments tell us that the current short-term trend is definitively lower on this weekly

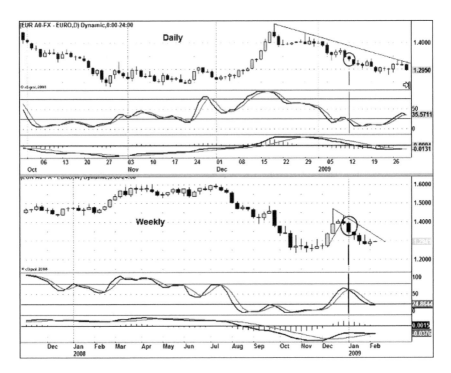

Figure 13-1 Short-Term Trends on Both Weekly and Daily EURUSD Charts Pointed Lower

chart. The daily chart in the upper panel highlights Monday, January 12, 2009, when the short-term trend is also lower on the basis of the current trendline and the positioning of the stochastic. This market, which is EURUSD, qualifies as one in which we can look for sell signals because of the coordination of both of those short-term trends.

The intraday charts in Figure 13-2 are from Tuesday, January 13, 2009. We knew before this day started that it qualified as one in which we would be looking to take sell signals.

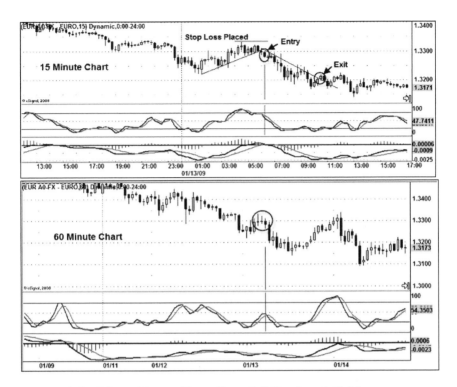

Figure 13-2 Fifteen-Minute Chart Gives Sell Signal, and 60-Minute Chart Confirms

On the 15-minute chart in the upper panel in Figure 13-2 we see a sell signal marked "Entry" that coincides with a change-of-direction candle that also broke the previous short-term uptrend. This occurrence, coupled with a second stochastic cross down in the past one and a half hours, provided a nice sell signal. Before initiating a short position, we would make sure that the behavior on the 60-minute chart in the lower panel in Figure 13-2 confirmed a possible price shift. We see on the 60-minute chart that we have first a shooting star, then an inside candle, then a close below the inside candle, and then a stochastic trigger line cross, all of which constitutes bearish behavior and confirms the sell signal on the 15-minute chart. In other words, we use the higher time frame chart, in this case the 60-minute chart, to both filter and confirm the signal on the 15-minute chart. Once we are in the short position, we want to place a buy stop-loss order above the last swing high in case the market shifts back higher or in case there is an unforeseen

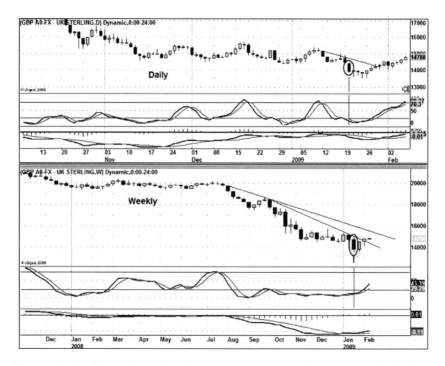

Figure 13-3 Short-Term Trends on the Weekly and Daily GBPUSD Charts Pointed Lower

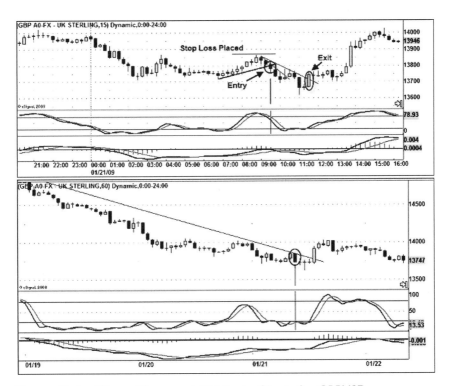

Figure 13-4 Fifteen-Minute and 60-Minute Charts for GBPUSD

development that could have an adverse effect on our trade (position). Once we exit the trade after a close above the last short-term trendline combined with a bull cross of the stochastic above the oversold line, we need to remember to cancel that buy stop.

In the trade example in Figures 13-3 and 13-4, we again see that the short-term trends on our weekly and daily charts are pointed lower. That indicates that we will be looking for sell signals in GBPUSD on the 15-minute chart if the 60-minute chart confirms.

In the two charts in Figure 13-3 we have both short-term trends pointed lower for the highlighted candles. The weekly candle starts on January 19, 2008, and the daily chart highlights the January 20, 2009, candle; the intraday charts in Figure 13-4 are from January 21, 2009. We see in the intraday charts how we had a setup and a signal on the 15-minute chart and at the same time had a downtrend in the 60-minute chart. We also had significant positive divergence on the 60-minute chart, which called for a discretionary decision. In this example we opted to take the signal on the basis of the weakness in the daily chart.

Also notice on the 15-minute chart in the upper panel in Figure 13-4 how we could have entered this trade one candle earlier if we had updated that small uptrend, or support line, by drawing it more tightly. Even with a tighter trendline we would have had a cross of the stochastic, which indicates a shift in momentum. At the time of the sell signal on the 15-minute chart, the 60-minute chart was in a clear downtrend, with the stochastic below its oversold line, indicating weakness. Contrary to the terms *oversold* and *overbought*, we consider it a sign of strength when the stochastic is above the 75 level and a sign of weakness when it is below the 25 level. In this instance price behavior on the 60-minute chart confirms the signal on the lower time frame 15-minute chart.

In our courses at www.Trading-U.com we spend a considerable amount of time teaching our students how to use higher time frame charts to filter and confirm trade signals on the lower time frames. The market in this example turned around quickly, and we would exit the trade on the basis of the combination of a trendline break and a stochastic cross above the oversold line. The fast turnaround in price points out why it is necessary to monitor trades closely and shows the importance of noting the divergence that had built up on the 60-minute chart. If you go back to the daily chart in Figure 13-3, you will see that despite falling prices, positive divergence had built up on that chart too.

Keeping a Trading Journal

As traders we don't always have the luxury of picking up the phone and calling or Skyping our mentor. We may not even have a mentor. Often we have to keep our own counsel, and the danger in that is, as the old saying goes, that "a lawyer who represents himself has a fool for a client." The way to avoid falling into the trap of making up excuses why you did not take a trade or why you exited a trade early or even lying to yourself about your actions and prospects is to keep a trading journal. It may sound like a stretch to be less than truthful about why you did what you did in your trading account, but we see it time and time again in our students when they trade on what they think is going to happen instead of on definitive signals that already have occurred or at least are unfolding. Another reason why 90 percent of speculative account holders lose money is the disconnect between what their trading plans tell their brains to do and what their brains tell their index fingers to do when clicking the mouse. If you fall into this trap, how are you going to fix it if you don't confront it? By writing these things down in your trading journal you will be shining a light on what's trying to stay in the shadows of your subconscious.

A trading journal is more than a depository for market observations and lessons and more than a place to record and check off the necessary conditions as dictated by a trading plan. Your trading journal is going to be your alter ego and your confessional. You can feel free to write down anything related to you whether it pertains to trading or not. Remember, trading is over 90 percent mental, meaning there is a lot going on in both your conscious mind and subconscious mind that will affect your trading in addition to what you see on the charts. You need to create an organized, supportive work environment in which to trade. Start planning to create this environment by writing out the blueprint in your trading journal. You need to maintain a focused and diligent mindset and be aware of the dangers of fast money and its intoxicating effects. Write down your thoughts and observations on this in your trading journal. You need to come to terms with your fears and make a thoughtful decision about whether trading is for you. Is trading worth the risk of both time and money?

Yes, you need to write down the conditions that existed on the chart and in the market when you sized up a trade and then entered your position. However, you also need to make it your job to put yourself and then keep yourself in a healthy place mentally before, during, and after trading, and your journal is going to help you do that. Nobody is as well suited to taking care of you as you are—for the most part. Things that you think and feel are going to come out in your journal, and by noting what comes out of the end of your pen, you are going to be aware of your concerns and plans and triumphs.

What you write in your trading journal is up to you. If there is one thing that should be mandatory, it is that every time you make a trade, whether a demo or live, you need to write down the following:

1. Market traded
2. Direction traded from
3. Date and time
4. Signals used
5. Time frame traded
6. Trend or countertrend

This is going to help you and your mentor see where you are in your current knowledge and, more important, help highlight any mistakes you have made. One of the backbones of the learning process at www.Trading-U.com is going over the demo trades the students make. The knowledge that every trade they make must be reviewed by an instructor has a positive effect on the students' trading because they take the exercise more seriously as they learn to focus on every detail of the process. We recommend that if you do not decide to participate in our mentorship programs, you at least try to get involved with a group of like-minded traders and insist on putting the information we've just listed in a spreadsheet and sending it to the other members of your group. Set up a time to pull up your charts and review your trades with a friend, candle by candle. Each trade you make will be slightly different from the last. There are a hundred variations of a setup. The only thing that can come close to having experience is reviewing a friend's trades candle by candle and seeing the same order of operation unfolding each time. You will learn how to filter trades and how to confirm trades, and that will improve your winning percentage and increase your confidence. All this is information you can write in your journal. Make sure to write down the occasions when you've made mistakes, because it is from mistakes and lapses that you will learn the most!

CONCLUSION

Mastering the Markets

The reason why few succeed and many fail is that the successful are armed with a tested plan. Have you ever sat in a classroom on the first day of a new school year and heard the instructor announce that statistically speaking, half the individuals in the room won't be around for the second half of the semester? After making this announcement, the instructor walks around the room slowly, looking at the students one by one. He very likely can tell by the students' reactions and postures who will be around and who won't. His announcement was based on statistical evidence, and his observations entail noting people's behavior and recalling his own experience. The student who sits up straight and smiles directly at the teacher very likely will make it. Her posture of "bring it on" and her smile show confidence. The student who slumps down while furrows of concern wrinkle his brow and turn down his mouth is on the bubble before the class even begins. With some students the instructor just can't tell.

Class for you has not begun yet. This book is an instructional text and provides a wide base for a structure you must build within yourself that has to get smaller yet stronger with every level added. You will need to take the information you have learned in this book and boil it down to a trading plan no more than two or three pages long. As you journey from novice to knowledgeable to accomplished, the lessons learned must be absorbed and applied and experienced until you intuitively know that they work. Once you have proved your trading plan's value to yourself through demo trading, you will be on your way to a subconscious understanding of what you are doing and will find that you can make judgments in seconds that used to take minutes. Eventually you will realize that for all the myriad lessons you've been taught, the tools studied and practiced, and the seriousness of the craft implanted, trading comes down to two simple actions: initiating the trade and exiting the trade.

The goal of this book is to ensure you that you will be around at the end of the semester. It also is designed to provide you with the essential lessons you will need to become a master discretionary trader.

BIBLIOGRAPHY

Boroden, Carolyn. *Fibonacci Trading*. New York: McGraw Hill, 2008.

Dalton, James, Eric Jones, and Robert Dalton. *Mind Over Markets*. Chicago: Probus, 1990.

Falloon, William. *Charlie D*. New York: Wiley, 1997.

Fischer, Robert. *Fibonacci Applications and Strategies for Traders*. New York: Wiley, 1993.

Gann, W.D. *How to Make Profits Trading in Commodities*. Pomeroy, WA: Lambert–Gann, 1942.

Goodspeed, Bennett. *The Tao-Jones Averages*. New York: Penguin Books, 1984.

Kase, Cynthia. *Trading with the Odds*. New York: McGraw Hill, 1995.

Kirkpatrick, Charles, and Julie Dahlquist. *Technical Analysis*. Upper Saddle River, NJ: FT Press, 2007.

LeFevre, Edwin. *Reminiscences of a Stock Operator*. New York: The Sun Dial Press, Inc., 1938.

Lipton, Bruce. *The Biology of Believe*. Santa Rosa, CA: Elite Books, 2005.

293

Mandelbrot, Benoit, and Richard Hudson. *The (Mis)Behavior of Markets*. New York: Basic Books, 2004.

Murphy, John. *Technical Analysis of the Futures Markets*. New York: New York Institute of Finance, 1986.

Person, John. *A Complete Guide to Technical Trading Tactics*. Hoboken, NJ: Wiley, 2004.

Rhea, Robert. *The Dow Theory*. New York: Barrons, 1932. Reprint New York: Fraser, 1993.

Sperandeo, Victor. *Trader Vic—Methods of a Wall Street Master*. New York: Wiley, 1993.

Williams, Bill, and Justine Gregory-Williams. *Trading Chaos*. 2nd ed. Hoboken, NJ: Wiley, 2004.

INDEX

ABOUT THE AUTHORS

Jay Norris is a senior market strategist and trading instructor for Brewer FX in Chicago. He worked on the trading floor of the Chicago Board of Trade throughout the 1980s and 1990s in various roles before moving to the customer side of the business in 2001. He has published several articles about trading in *Technical Analysis of Stocks & Commodities* magazine. Mr. Norris lives in Chicago.

Al Gaskill is an independent trader, an instructor, and a principal in Brewer Investment Group. Mr. Gaskill lives in Florida.

Teresa Bell is an educator for www.Trading-u.com. Ms. Bell lives in Chicago.